Holistic Architecture - Designing Spaces for Wellness

Anelly Aya

Introduction to Holistic Architecture

In the realm of architectural design, a paradigm shift is occurring—one that transcends the mere physicality of structures to embrace a holistic approach focused on enhancing human well-being. This transformation is encapsulated in the burgeoning discipline of Holistic Architecture, an exciting frontier where form and function unite to create spaces that nurture mind, body, and spirit.

Understanding the Essence

At its core, Holistic Architecture represents a departure from conventional design philosophies. It extends beyond aesthetics and functionality, delving into the profound interconnectedness between individuals and their surroundings. The built environment, in this context, is not merely a backdrop but an active participant in shaping the human experience. The fundamental premise is to craft spaces that promote health, harmony, and happiness.

Balancing Physical and Emotional Needs

The journey into Holistic Architecture begins with a profound consideration of human needs. Beyond the basics of shelter, this approach recognizes the importance of emotional and psychological well-being. Spaces are conceived not only to fulfill utilitarian purposes but to evoke positive emotions and foster a sense of connection. By understanding the symbiotic relationship between architecture and human psychology, designers can create environments that resonate with the occupants on a profound level.

Integration of Nature

One of the key pillars of Holistic Architecture is the seamless integration of nature into the built environment. This goes beyond incorporating greenery or using natural materials; it involves creating a symbiotic relationship between the indoors and the outdoors. Biophilic design principles guide architects in bringing the healing power of nature into urban spaces, promoting a sense of calm and rejuvenation. Whether through expansive windows framing scenic views or interior gardens that breathe life into enclosed spaces, the goal is to reconnect individuals with the natural world.

Holistic Materials and Sustainability

Another critical facet of Holistic Architecture is the conscious selection of materials. Beyond aesthetics and durability, the focus is on materials that contribute to the overall well-being of both occupants and the planet. Sustainable materials, those that are environmentally friendly and have minimal impact, take precedence. The ethos of holistic design extends to the life cycle of materials, considering their production, use, and eventual disposal.

Mindful Space Planning

In the pursuit of holistic well-being, the layout and organization of space play a pivotal role. Mindful space planning involves a deliberate consideration of how spaces flow and interact. It's about creating environments that facilitate positive human interactions, inspire creativity, and provide areas for both social engagement and solitary reflection. The design goes beyond aesthetics, seeking a balance that supports the diverse needs and activities of the occupants.

Harmony in Diversity

Holistic Architecture embraces diversity in its myriad forms. It recognizes that individuals have unique preferences, needs, and cultural backgrounds. A truly holistic space is one that accommodates this diversity, creating an inclusive environment where everyone feels welcome. The design adapts to varying lifestyles and preferences, fostering a sense of belonging and unity within the built environment.

Setting the Tone for the Journey Ahead

As we embark on this exploration of Holistic Architecture, it is essential to recognize that it represents more than a design trend; it signifies a profound shift in our approach to the spaces we inhabit. This journey takes us beyond the conventional boundaries of architecture, encouraging us to see spaces not just as structures but as integral components of our lives.

Summary

The introductory chapter sets the stage for a deep dive into the world of Holistic Architecture, a discipline that transcends traditional design paradigms. Holistic Architecture is about creating spaces that go beyond functionality, embracing a profound understanding of the interconnectedness between individuals and their built environment. It encompasses mindful space planning, the integration of nature, and the use of sustainable materials to craft environments that prioritize emotional and psychological well-being. As we navigate through the subsequent chapters, we will explore the various facets of this transformative approach and understand how it can revolutionize the way we perceive and interact with the spaces around us.

The Intersection of Architecture and Well-being

In the ever-evolving tapestry of architectural discourse, an increasingly prominent thread weaves through the fabric—the profound connection between architecture and well-being. This chapter delves into the intricate interplay of these two realms, exploring how the design of our built environment can significantly impact our physical, mental, and emotional health.

Architectural Alchemy: Transforming Spaces into Sanctuaries

The built environment, often viewed through the lens of function and aesthetics, is now becoming a canvas for architects to paint a picture of wellness. The concept of well-being transcends the absence of illness; it encompasses a state of holistic health, encompassing physical vitality, mental clarity, and emotional equilibrium. Architects are emerging as alchemists, blending design elements to create spaces that nurture, heal, and inspire.

Biophilia: Nature as a Healing Elixir

At the heart of the intersection between architecture and well-being lies the concept of biophilia—a deep, instinctive bond between humans and nature. This intrinsic connection, hardwired into our evolutionary history, forms the basis for designing spaces that echo the natural world. From incorporating living green walls to maximizing natural light, architects employ biophilic principles to evoke the serenity and vitality associated with natural environments.

Lighting the Path to Wellness

Natural light, a timeless protagonist in architectural narratives, assumes a central role in promoting well-being. Beyond its practical illumination, sunlight harbors a spectrum of benefits—enhanced mood, improved circadian rhythms, and the synthesis of vitamin D. Architects, recognizing the pivotal role of light in health, are embracing designs that prioritize ample daylight penetration while balancing it with strategic artificial lighting to create harmonious, well-lit spaces.

Air Quality: Breathing Life into Design

In the pursuit of wellness, the quality of the air we breathe within our spaces is paramount. Architectural choices can either support or hinder respiratory health. Ventilation systems, material selections, and the integration of greenery all contribute to indoor air quality. The conscientious architect considers these factors, ensuring that occupants not only inhabit aesthetically pleasing spaces but also breathe air that invigorates rather than compromises health.

Designing for Mental Respite

The architectural environment has a profound impact on mental well-being. Spaces designed for mental respite prioritize tranquility, privacy, and opportunities for introspection. Whether crafting serene corners in bustling urban environments or conceiving buildings with thoughtful spatial flow, architects contribute to mental wellness by creating havens that provide moments of calm in the midst of life's frenetic pace.

Holistic Spatial Flow

The layout of a space can influence how people move, interact, and experience the environment. Holistic spatial flow involves intentional design to promote a sense of coherence and harmony. Architects strategically plan the arrangement of rooms, corridors, and communal areas to facilitate both social engagement and moments of solitude, catering to diverse human needs and fostering a sense of community within a physical setting.

Soundscapes: Orchestrating Harmony

In the symphony of architecture and well-being, sound plays a pivotal role. Thoughtful consideration of acoustics is integral to creating spaces that promote concentration, relaxation, and a sense of well-being. Whether it's minimizing noise in work environments, incorporating natural sounds in recreational spaces, or designing buildings with acoustic materials that enhance auditory comfort, architects orchestrate soundscapes that contribute to overall wellness.

Summary

This chapter has illuminated the intricate dance between architecture and well-being, revealing how the design of our surroundings can be a powerful determinant of our physical, mental, and emotional health. From the incorporation of biophilic principles to the strategic use of natural light, architects are forging spaces that transcend functionality to become sanctuaries for well-being. As we navigate through the subsequent chapters, we will continue to unravel the multifaceted relationship between architecture and wellness, exploring innovative design approaches that prioritize the health and happiness of those who inhabit these thoughtfully crafted spaces.

The Power of Purposeful Design

In the realm of architecture, purposeful design emerges as a guiding principle that transcends aesthetics and functionality. This chapter delves into the profound impact of purposeful design on the built environment, exploring how intentionality in architectural decisions can shape spaces to enhance well-being, foster a sense of meaning, and contribute to the overall quality of life for occupants.

The Essence of Purposeful Design

At its core, purposeful design in architecture is an intentional and thoughtful approach that goes beyond the superficial aspects of form and structure. It involves a conscious consideration of the intended use, the needs of the occupants, and the broader context in which the building exists. Purposeful design acknowledges that every element within a space, from the layout to the choice of materials, has the potential to influence the human experience.

Creating Meaningful Spaces

Purposeful design is not just about creating visually appealing structures; it is about imbuing spaces with meaning. A purposefully designed environment engages its occupants on a deeper level, resonating with their values, culture, and aspirations. This might involve incorporating symbolic elements, cultural references, or historical narratives into the architectural fabric, creating spaces that tell a story and evoke a sense of connection.

User-Centered Design: Beyond Form to Function

The power of purposeful design is most evident when the needs and experiences of the end-users take center stage. User-centered design principles prioritize the human experience, considering how people will interact with and navigate through a space. Architects engage with future occupants to understand their habits, preferences, and aspirations, ensuring that the design not only serves its functional purpose but also enhances the well-being of those who inhabit it.

Spatial Flow and Functionality

In purposeful design, spatial flow is carefully orchestrated to align with the intended functions of the space. Whether it's a residential dwelling, a workspace, or a communal area, the layout is meticulously planned to optimize usability and efficiency. Spaces are organized with a keen understanding of how people move within them, fostering both practical functionality and a sense of coherence.

Sustainability as a Design Imperative

Purposeful design extends beyond the immediate needs of occupants to embrace a broader environmental consciousness. Sustainable design practices are integral to purposeful architecture, considering the long-term impact of buildings on the planet. From energy-efficient systems to the use of eco-friendly materials, purposeful design acknowledges the responsibility architects bear in minimizing the environmental footprint of their creations.

Adaptable Spaces for Changing Needs

The dynamism of life requires spaces that can adapt to evolving needs. Purposeful design anticipates future changes, whether in the function of a space or the demographics of its occupants. Flexibility and adaptability are woven into the architectural DNA, allowing spaces to evolve over time without losing their fundamental utility or aesthetic appeal.

Emotional Impact and Well-being

The emotional impact of architectural design should not be underestimated. Purposeful design recognizes that the built environment can evoke a wide spectrum of emotions—from tranquility and joy to inspiration and introspection. By intentionally curating the atmosphere within a space, architects contribute to the emotional well-being of its occupants, fostering positive experiences and a sense of belonging.

Innovations in Purposeful Design

As the architectural landscape evolves, so too do the tools and techniques available to designers. Innovations such as parametric design, virtual reality simulations, and artificial intelligence are harnessed to inform purposeful design. These technologies enable architects to visualize and optimize spaces in ways that were previously unimaginable, allowing for a more precise and tailored approach to creating environments that serve their purpose effectively.

Summary

This chapter has explored the transformative influence of purposeful design in architecture, emphasizing the intentionality behind every decision in the creation of built environments. Purposeful design goes beyond aesthetics, embracing a holistic approach that considers the needs of occupants, the environmental impact, and the emotional resonance of a space. As we proceed through the subsequent chapters, we will continue to unravel the layers of purposeful design, examining its role in shaping spaces that not only serve practical functions but also enrich the lives of those who inhabit them.

Integrating Nature into Built Environments

In the dance between the urban and the natural, architects are increasingly recognizing the profound impact that nature can have on the well-being of individuals within built environments. This chapter delves into the art and science of integrating nature into architectural design, exploring how the symbiotic relationship between the constructed and the organic can transform spaces into havens of tranquility, vitality, and inspiration.

Biophilia: The Heartbeat of Holistic Design

At the core of integrating nature into built environments lies the concept of biophilia—an innate human tendency to seek connections with nature and other forms of life. This principle, articulated by biologist E.O. Wilson, has become a guiding light for architects seeking to infuse their designs with the life-affirming qualities of the natural world. Biophilic design goes beyond the incorporation of mere greenery; it seeks to create environments that echo the patterns, textures, and rhythms of nature, fostering a deep sense of well-being among occupants.

Green Roofs and Living Walls: Vertical Gardens in Urban Oases

One of the tangible expressions of biophilic design is the integration of green roofs and living walls into urban landscapes. Green roofs, adorned with vegetation, not only provide insulation and reduce energy consumption but also offer a retreat for the eyes in densely built cityscapes. Living walls, vertical installations of plants, contribute to air purification and bring a touch of nature to otherwise sterile surfaces. Together, these features transform concrete jungles into vibrant, living spaces.

Maximizing Natural Light: The Architecture of Illumination

Nature's most powerful element, sunlight, takes center stage in the integration of nature into built environments. Architects strategically design spaces to maximize natural light, promoting a connection with the outdoors and harnessing the health benefits associated with exposure to sunlight. From expansive windows framing scenic views to innovative skylights that bring daylight into interior spaces, the architecture of illumination becomes a conduit for nature to permeate the built environment.

Courtyards and Atriums: Nurturing Nature in the Heart of Structures

Courtyards and atriums emerge as architectural canvases where nature can be intricately woven into the fabric of buildings. These open, central spaces not only provide a visual connection with the sky but also offer opportunities for lush landscaping. Architects use these areas to introduce water features, plant life, and natural materials, creating microcosms of nature that serve as communal gathering spots and focal points for contemplation.

Biophilic Materials: Touching Nature in the Built Form

Beyond visual and spatial elements, the integration of nature into built environments extends to the materials used in construction. Biophilic materials mimic the textures and aesthetics of the natural world, creating a sensory connection with the environment. Wood, stone, and other organic materials not only contribute to the visual appeal of spaces but also engage the sense of touch, grounding occupants in a tactile experience that resonates with the natural elements.

Nature-Inspired Patterns and Motifs

Architects adept in biophilic design often draw inspiration from the intricate patterns and motifs found in nature. From fractals to leaf-like shapes, these elements are seamlessly integrated into the design of structures, interiors, and furnishings. Nature-inspired patterns create a visual rhythm that echoes the harmony found in the natural world, evoking a sense of balance and order within the built environment.

Water Features: Fluidity and Serenity

The inclusion of water features within built environments adds a dynamic and sensory layer to architectural design. Whether manifested as fountains, ponds, or cascading water walls, these features not only contribute to the aesthetic appeal but also induce a calming effect. The sound of flowing water has been shown to reduce stress and enhance well-being, making water features a powerful tool in creating holistic and tranquil spaces.

Urban Parks and Natural Reserves: Expanding Nature's Domain

In the pursuit of integrating nature into the urban fabric, architects are increasingly championing the creation of urban parks and natural reserves. These green lungs within the cityscape serve as communal spaces for recreation, relaxation, and connection with nature. Thoughtfully designed pathways, seating areas, and recreational facilities blend seamlessly with the natural surroundings, offering a respite from the hustle and bustle of urban life.

Educational and Therapeutic Gardens: Nurturing Minds and Bodies

Architects engaged in biophilic design are extending its benefits to educational and healthcare environments. Educational gardens provide students with hands-on learning experiences, fostering an appreciation for the natural world. Therapeutic gardens, designed with healing in mind, offer patients in healthcare facilities a serene outdoor environment that complements medical interventions, contributing to their physical and mental well-being.

Summary

This chapter has explored the transformative integration of nature into built environments, a process guided by the principles of biophilia. From green roofs and living walls to the strategic use of natural light, water features, and nature-inspired design elements, architects are weaving the vitality of the natural world into the very fabric of structures. As we journey through the subsequent chapters, the exploration will deepen, uncovering innovative ways in which nature and architecture coalesce to create spaces that not only shelter but also uplift and rejuvenate the human spirit.

Mindful Space Planning for Harmony

In the symphony of architecture, the art of mindful space planning emerges as a conductor, orchestrating a harmonious relationship between form, function, and the well-being of occupants. This chapter delves into the nuances of mindful space planning, exploring how intentional and thoughtful spatial design can create environments that foster harmony, balance, and a sense of connection.

The Essence of Mindful Space Planning

Mindful space planning is an approach that transcends mere functionality, considering how spaces influence human behavior, emotions, and interactions. At its core, it involves a deliberate and conscious effort to craft environments that are not only aesthetically pleasing but also responsive to the diverse needs and activities of the occupants. The essence lies in creating spaces that resonate with the human experience, promoting a sense of balance and coherence.

Holistic Human-Centric Design

Central to mindful space planning is a deep understanding of the people who will inhabit a space. Human-centric design principles guide architects to consider the diverse needs, preferences, and behaviors of occupants. This approach recognizes that spaces are not static entities but dynamic environments that should adapt to the evolving requirements of individuals, fostering a sense of belonging and well-being.

Zoning for Functionality and Flow

Mindful space planning involves a thoughtful allocation of space based on functionality and flow. Different zones within a space are designated for specific activities, optimizing usability and efficiency. Whether it's creating dedicated areas for work, relaxation, or social interaction, architects strategically organize spaces to accommodate a variety of functions, ensuring that the flow is intuitive and enhances the overall user experience.

Openness and Enclosure: Striking a Balance

A delicate balance between openness and enclosure characterizes mindful space planning. Open layouts promote a sense of spaciousness and foster social interaction, while strategically placed enclosures provide privacy and defined areas for specific activities. Architects navigate this balance to create dynamic spaces that offer a sense of connection without sacrificing the need for individual retreats.

Adaptable Furnishings and Modular Design

The versatility of a space is enhanced through the incorporation of adaptable furnishings and modular design. Mindful space planning anticipates the changing needs of occupants over time and provides flexibility through furniture that can be easily reconfigured. Modular design allows for the adaptation of spaces, ensuring that they remain relevant and functional as requirements evolve.

Natural Traffic Flow: Navigating Spaces with Intuition

Mindful space planning takes into account the natural flow of human movement within a space. Thoughtful consideration is given to the arrangement of furniture, pathways, and points of interaction to create an intuitive and seamless traffic flow. Spaces are designed to minimize congestion and allow for easy navigation, enhancing the overall comfort and functionality of the environment.

Creating Zones of Tranquility and Inspiration

In the hustle and bustle of modern life, mindful space planning carves out zones dedicated to tranquility and inspiration. Whether it's a cozy reading nook bathed in natural light, a meditation corner surrounded by greenery, or an artfully designed workspace that sparks creativity, architects curate environments that cater to the diverse emotional and psychological needs of occupants.

Maximizing Natural Light and Views

The integration of natural light and expansive views into space planning is a hallmark of mindful design. Architects strategically position windows and openings to maximize daylight penetration, reducing reliance on artificial lighting and promoting a connection with the outdoors. Views of nature, urban landscapes, or carefully curated elements contribute to a sense of openness and well-being within the space.

Multifunctional Spaces: Versatility in Design

Mindful space planning embraces the concept of multifunctionality. Spaces are designed to serve multiple purposes, adapting to the diverse activities and requirements of occupants. Whether it's a living room that transforms into a guest bedroom or a communal area that doubles as a workspace, architects weave versatility into the fabric of spaces, optimizing their utility and relevance.

Technological Integration: Seamless and Purposeful

In the digital age, mindful space planning incorporates technology seamlessly and purposefully. From integrated smart home systems to flexible workspaces equipped with cutting-edge technology, architects leverage advancements to enhance the functionality and connectivity of spaces. The goal is to integrate technology in a way that augments the human experience without overshadowing the natural harmony of the environment.

Summary

Mindful space planning is the virtuoso conductor in the architectural symphony, orchestrating a harmonious relationship between form, function, and the well-being of occupants. This chapter has delved into the essence of mindful space planning, exploring its human-centric design principles, its careful balance between openness and enclosure, and its focus on adaptability and versatility. As we move forward, we will continue our exploration, uncovering innovative approaches and case studies that showcase the transformative power of thoughtful spatial design in creating environments that resonate with the human spirit.

Biophilic Design: Enhancing Well-being with Nature

In the evolving landscape of architectural design, a profound shift towards reconnecting with nature has given rise to the concept of biophilic design. This chapter unravels the layers of biophilic design, exploring how architects are harnessing the healing power of nature to enhance well-being, foster creativity, and create environments that resonate with the innate human connection to the natural world.

Understanding Biophilic Design

Biophilic design, rooted in the concept of biophilia, is a design philosophy that seeks to integrate nature into the built environment. Coined by biologist E.O. Wilson, biophilia describes the innate human inclination to connect with nature and other living organisms. Biophilic design translates this concept into architectural practice, recognizing that incorporating natural elements into spaces can have profound positive effects on the well-being of occupants.

Nature in the Urban Jungle: Bringing the Outdoors In

In densely populated urban areas, the challenge is to create environments that provide a sense of nature despite the concrete surroundings. Biophilic design addresses this challenge by bringing the outdoors in. Large windows offering panoramic views, indoor plants, and natural materials like wood and stone serve as conduits for nature to permeate the urban built environment. This not only enhances aesthetics but also contributes to a healthier and more enjoyable living or working experience.

Biophilic Elements: Beyond Aesthetics

Biophilic design goes beyond superficial aesthetics; it involves a thoughtful incorporation of specific elements that mimic patterns and processes found in nature. The use of fractals, which are repetitive geometric patterns found in leaves, flowers, and clouds, can be seen in architectural details, carpets, or wall designs. Water features, reminiscent of natural rivers or ponds, contribute not only to visual appeal but also to the auditory and tactile experiences within a space.

The Impact of Natural Light: A Vital Element

One of the most powerful elements in biophilic design is natural light. Sunlight, with its dynamic qualities, not only illuminates spaces but also influences the circadian rhythm, affecting mood, sleep patterns, and overall well-being. Architects strategically design spaces to maximize daylight penetration, ensuring that occupants are bathed in natural light. Light wells, skylights, and expansive windows become instruments in orchestrating the play of sunlight within the built environment.

Biophilic Patterns in Architecture

Architects draw inspiration from the rich tapestry of natural patterns when integrating biophilic design. The branching patterns of trees, the spirals found in seashells, or the intricate symmetry seen in flowers are replicated in architectural elements. These patterns, when seamlessly integrated into buildings, create a visual harmony that resonates with the order and beauty found in the natural world.

Embracing the Seasons: Dynamic Environments

Biophilic design recognizes the ever-changing beauty of nature throughout the seasons. Architects design spaces that allow occupants to experience these natural shifts. Whether through strategically placed windows framing seasonal views or outdoor spaces that adapt to different weather conditions, the goal is to create dynamic environments that engage occupants with the ebb and flow of the natural world.

Biophilic Design in Workspaces: Boosting Productivity and Well-being

The application of biophilic design principles in workspaces has gained prominence, driven by the desire to enhance employee well-being and productivity. Incorporating natural elements such as indoor plants, green walls, and views of nature into office spaces has been shown to reduce stress, improve focus, and foster a sense of well-being among employees. Workspaces designed with biophilic principles become environments where creativity and innovation flourish.

Restorative Environments: Nature as a Healing Balm

Biophilic design extends its influence to environments dedicated to healing, such as hospitals and wellness centers. Nature-inspired elements, soothing colors, and the integration of natural materials contribute to creating restorative spaces that aid in the healing process. Views of nature, even if simulated through images or videos, have been proven to have positive effects on patients' recovery.

Educational Spaces: Nurturing Young Minds

In educational settings, biophilic design contributes to creating environments that support the learning process. Classrooms with ample natural light, outdoor learning spaces, and the incorporation of nature-themed elements create settings where students feel more engaged and connected to their surroundings. Biophilic design in educational spaces not only enhances academic performance but also fosters a love for the natural world.

Biophilic Residential Design: Creating Homes in Harmony with Nature

Residential spaces designed with biophilic principles become sanctuaries that seamlessly integrate with the natural environment. Indoor-outdoor living spaces, private gardens, and the use of natural materials evoke a sense of tranquility and connection to nature. Biophilic homes provide a retreat from the demands of modern life, offering residents a space where they can recharge and find solace.

Challenges and Considerations in Biophilic Design

While biophilic design offers a myriad of benefits, it comes with its own set of challenges. Integrating nature into urban environments requires thoughtful planning and may be limited by space constraints. Maintaining living elements, such as indoor plants, necessitates ongoing care. Overcoming these challenges involves a commitment to the principles of biophilic design and creative solutions that adapt to the specific context and constraints of each project.

Summary

Biophilic design emerges as a transformative force in architecture, reconnecting individuals with the inherent beauty and healing power of nature. This chapter has explored the principles and applications of biophilic design, from bringing the outdoors into urban spaces to its impact on work environments, healing spaces, educational settings, and residential design. As we proceed, we will continue our journey through the evolving landscape of architectural innovation, uncovering how biophilic design continues to shape spaces that not only serve practical functions but also elevate the human experience.

Sustainable Materials and Their Impact on Health

In the pursuit of creating healthier, more environmentally conscious built environments, architects are increasingly turning to sustainable materials. This chapter delves into the significance of incorporating sustainable materials into architectural design, exploring their impact on both the well-being of occupants and the broader health of the planet.

The Imperative of Sustainability

Sustainable materials in architecture are not merely a trend; they represent a fundamental shift towards responsible and eco-friendly practices. The imperative of sustainability arises from the acknowledgment that traditional construction methods and materials contribute significantly to environmental degradation. Sustainable materials aim to mitigate this impact by considering the full life cycle of a material, from extraction and production to use and disposal.

Holistic Health: From Buildings to Occupants

The impact of sustainable materials on health is multifaceted, encompassing both the health of the occupants within a building and the health of the larger ecosystem. As architects embrace materials that are environmentally responsible, energy-efficient, and non-toxic, they contribute to a built environment that promotes holistic well-being.

Low Environmental Impact: Reducing Carbon Footprints

Sustainable materials are characterized by a low environmental impact throughout their life cycle. This begins with responsible sourcing, opting for materials that are renewable, recycled, or locally available to reduce transportation-related carbon emissions. Additionally, sustainable materials often require fewer resources and less energy in their production, minimizing their overall environmental footprint.

Indoor Air Quality: Breathing Easier

One of the direct impacts of sustainable materials on occupant health is the improvement of indoor air quality. Traditional building materials, such as certain paints, adhesives, and treated wood, can emit harmful pollutants known as volatile organic compounds (VOCs). Sustainable materials, often low in VOCs or VOC-free, contribute to healthier indoor air, reducing the risk of respiratory issues and other health concerns.

Biodegradability and Recyclability: Closing the Loop

Sustainable materials are designed with the end in mind, emphasizing biodegradability and recyclability. Unlike conventional materials that contribute to landfill waste, sustainable materials can be recycled or decomposed at the end of their life cycle. This closed-loop approach aligns with the principles of a circular economy, minimizing waste and supporting a regenerative relationship with the environment.

Renewable Energy: Powering Sustainable Production

The use of sustainable materials is closely linked to the adoption of renewable energy sources in their production processes. Manufacturers committed to sustainability often invest in solar, wind, or other renewable energy sources to power their operations. This not only reduces the carbon footprint of the materials but also aligns with the broader goals of transitioning to a cleaner and more sustainable energy future.

Wood as a Sustainable Marvel

Wood stands out as a prominent example of a sustainable material with numerous environmental and health benefits. Sourced responsibly, wood is renewable and has a lower carbon footprint compared to many other construction materials. It also has natural thermal properties, contributing to energy efficiency in buildings. Furthermore, exposure to wooden surfaces has been associated with positive physiological and psychological effects on occupants.

Innovations in Sustainable Materials

The realm of sustainable materials is continually evolving, driven by innovations that push the boundaries of eco-friendly design. From the development of bioplastics derived from renewable resources to the use of mycelium in construction materials, architects are exploring unconventional yet highly sustainable alternatives. These innovations not only address environmental concerns but also contribute to the creation of healthier indoor environments.

Local Sourcing and Community Impact

Sustainable materials often go hand in hand with a commitment to local sourcing. By utilizing materials that are available regionally, architects reduce the environmental impact associated with transportation while also fostering community resilience. This approach strengthens local economies, promotes regional biodiversity, and contributes to a more sustainable and interconnected built environment.

Certifications and Standards: Navigating the Landscape

Navigating the landscape of sustainable materials involves an understanding of certifications and standards. Various organizations, such as the Forest Stewardship Council (FSC) and the Cradle to Cradle Products Innovation Institute, provide certifications that validate the sustainability credentials of materials. Architects committed to sustainable design often seek out products with these certifications to ensure that they align with the highest environmental and health standards.

Cost Considerations and Long-Term Savings

While sustainable materials may sometimes have a higher upfront cost, the long-term savings they offer cannot be overlooked. Energy-efficient materials contribute to reduced operational costs over a building's lifespan. Additionally, the environmental and health benefits associated with sustainable materials can lead to lower healthcare costs for occupants, making a compelling case for the economic viability of sustainable architecture.

Public Awareness and Consumer Demand

As public awareness of environmental issues grows, there is an increasing demand for sustainable and eco-friendly products, including building materials. Architects responding to this demand not only contribute to a more sustainable industry but also align with the values of an environmentally conscious clientele. The integration of sustainable materials becomes a marker of responsible and forward-thinking architectural practices.

Challenges and Opportunities

Despite the progress made in the realm of sustainable materials, challenges persist. Limited availability of certain sustainable materials, cost considerations, and the need for further research into the long-term impacts of new materials are among the challenges architects face. However, these challenges also present opportunities for continued innovation, collaboration, and the development of more sustainable practices within the construction industry.

Summary

The integration of sustainable materials into architectural design emerges as a powerful force in promoting holistic health—from the well-being of occupants to the health of the planet. This chapter has explored the imperative of sustainability, the impact of sustainable materials on indoor air quality, and their role in reducing carbon footprints. From renewable energy in production to the transformative potential of wood as a sustainable marvel, architects are navigating a landscape of innovation and responsibility. As we move forward, the journey into sustainable architecture continues, unraveling new possibilities and contributing to a built environment that nurtures both people and the planet.

Light and Air: Optimizing Indoor Environments

In the intricate tapestry of architectural design, two fundamental elements, light, and air, emerge as pivotal forces shaping the well-being of occupants within indoor spaces. This chapter delves into the profound impact of optimizing light and air in architectural design, exploring how thoughtful integration of these elements contributes not only to the visual and physical comfort of inhabitants but also to their mental and emotional well-being.

The Essence of Natural Light

Natural light, with its dynamic qualities and ever-changing character, stands as a cornerstone in creating visually engaging and healthy indoor environments. Architects have long recognized the transformative power of natural light, which extends far beyond mere illumination. The quality and quantity of light in a space influence circadian rhythms, mood, and overall physiological well-being.

Harnessing Daylight: Strategies for Illumination

Architects strategically harness daylight to illuminate indoor spaces, reducing reliance on artificial lighting. The orientation of windows, the use of skylights, and the incorporation of light wells are all design strategies aimed at maximizing the penetration of natural light. This not only contributes to energy efficiency but also provides occupants with a connection to the external environment, fostering a sense of vitality and well-being.

Circadian Rhythms and Well-being

Optimizing natural light exposure within indoor spaces is essential for regulating circadian rhythms, the internal biological clock that influences various physiological processes. Exposure to natural light, especially in the morning, helps synchronize the body's internal clock with the external environment. This synchronization has been linked to improved sleep quality, enhanced mood, and overall well-being.

Balancing Glare and Comfort

While the benefits of natural light are vast, architects must also consider potential challenges, such as glare. Excessive brightness and glare can create discomfort and hinder visual tasks. Thoughtful design involves implementing shading devices, such as blinds or overhangs, and selecting glazing materials with appropriate tinting or coatings to strike a balance between maximizing daylight and ensuring visual comfort.

Artificial Lighting: Enhancing Comfort and Functionality

In spaces where natural light alone may not suffice, architects turn to artificial lighting to complement and enhance the overall lighting scheme. The key is to design lighting systems that mimic the qualities of natural light as closely as possible. Tunable LED lighting, for instance, allows for adjustments in color temperature throughout the day, contributing to circadian rhythm regulation and maintaining a connection to natural lighting patterns.

Air Quality: A Breath of Fresh Design

Just as crucial as light, the quality of indoor air plays a vital role in shaping the health and comfort of occupants. Indoor air can be laden with pollutants, such as volatile organic compounds (VOCs), particulate matter, and allergens. Architects employ strategies to optimize ventilation and air circulation, ensuring that indoor spaces are not only well-lit but also provide a continuous supply of fresh, clean air.

Natural Ventilation: Balancing Comfort and Energy Efficiency

Natural ventilation is an architectural strategy that utilizes natural airflow to provide fresh air and regulate indoor temperatures. This approach not only contributes to energy efficiency but also enhances the overall comfort and health of occupants. Strategies may include the strategic placement of operable windows, the use of atria for stack ventilation, and the incorporation of passive ventilation systems.

Mechanical Ventilation Systems: Precision in Airflow

In environments where natural ventilation may be insufficient, mechanical ventilation systems come into play. These systems are designed to deliver precise amounts of fresh air while efficiently removing indoor pollutants. The integration of high-quality air filtration systems ensures that indoor air remains free from contaminants, contributing to a healthier and more comfortable indoor environment.

Biophilic Design and Air Quality

The principles of biophilic design, which emphasize the connection between humans and nature, extend to indoor air quality. The integration of indoor plants not only enhances visual appeal but also contributes to improved air quality by naturally filtering pollutants. This biophilic approach aligns with the broader goal of creating indoor environments that support both physical and psychological well-being.

Thermal Comfort: The Marriage of Light and Air

The optimization of indoor environments involves finding the delicate balance between thermal comfort and the benefits of natural light and fresh air. Efficient insulation, proper shading, and the strategic placement of windows all play roles in creating spaces where occupants feel comfortable, with an ideal balance between illumination, ventilation, and temperature control.

Occupant Productivity and Well-being

The optimization of light and air within indoor spaces has profound implications for occupant productivity and overall well-being. A well-lit and well-ventilated space fosters a conducive environment for work, learning, and relaxation. Studies have shown that exposure to natural light and good indoor air quality positively influences cognitive function, creativity, and emotional well-being, contributing to a more vibrant and productive atmosphere.

Designing for Diverse Environments

Architects face the challenge of designing spaces that cater to diverse environments and occupant needs. A thoughtful approach involves understanding the specific requirements of each space—whether it's an office, a healthcare facility, or a residential setting—and tailoring the design to optimize both light and air in a way that enhances the functionality and well-being of the occupants.

Technology and Smart Building Solutions

Advancements in technology offer architects a toolkit for optimizing light and air in ways that were previously unimaginable. Smart building solutions, including sensors and automated systems, enable real-time monitoring and adjustment of lighting, ventilation, and air quality. These technologies contribute to energy efficiency, occupant comfort, and the overall sustainability of built environments.

Challenges and Future Directions

Optimizing light and air in indoor environments is not without its challenges. Urban density, limited access to natural ventilation, and the need for energy efficiency pose ongoing considerations for architects. However, these challenges also drive innovation, pushing architects to explore new solutions, technologies, and design strategies that address both current and emerging issues.

Summary

The optimization of light and air within indoor environments emerges as a dynamic and multi-faceted endeavor in architectural design. This chapter has explored the transformative impact of natural light on circadian rhythms and well-being, the strategies for balancing glare and comfort, and the significance of air quality in creating healthy indoor spaces. As architects continue to navigate the interplay between light, air, and design, the journey unfolds towards creating environments that not only illuminate and ventilate but also inspire and elevate the human experience.

Creating Tranquil Retreats within Urban Spaces

In the bustling heart of urban landscapes, where the rhythm of city life can be both invigorating and overwhelming, architects are weaving a narrative of tranquility. This chapter delves into the art of creating tranquil retreats within urban spaces, exploring how thoughtful design, strategic landscaping, and innovative concepts can carve out sanctuaries amidst the urban hustle, offering respite and rejuvenation to inhabitants.

The Urban Conundrum

Urban living is synonymous with vibrancy, opportunities, and connectivity. However, it often comes at the cost of tranquility, as the constant hum of traffic, the frenetic pace of activities, and the towering structures create an environment that can be both exhilarating and exhausting. Recognizing the need for balance, architects are embracing the challenge of integrating serene retreats seamlessly into the urban fabric.

Designing for Mindful Escapes

Creating tranquil retreats within urban spaces requires a mindful approach to design that goes beyond aesthetics. Architects delve into the psychology of relaxation, drawing inspiration from nature, incorporating elements that engage the senses, and crafting spaces that encourage mindfulness. The goal is to design environments that provide a mental escape from the urban chaos, fostering a sense of calm and rejuvenation.

Green Oases: The Power of Urban Greenery

The integration of greenery stands out as a foundational element in creating tranquil retreats within urban spaces. Pocket parks, rooftop gardens, and strategically placed trees contribute not only to the visual appeal but also to the psychological well-being of inhabitants. Greenery acts as a visual buffer, softening the harsh lines of urban infrastructure and introducing a touch of nature into the built environment.

Water Features: Calming Ripples in the Urban Landscape

Water, with its soothing and rhythmic qualities, becomes a powerful tool in crafting tranquil retreats. Urban water features, such as fountains, ponds, and water walls, not only add a visual spectacle but also create a calming acoustic backdrop. The presence of water introduces a multisensory experience, inviting inhabitants to pause, reflect, and find solace in the midst of urban activity.

Urban Courtyards and Pockets of Peace

Architects leverage the spatial intricacies of urban design to create hidden gems—intimate courtyards and pockets of peace nestled within the urban sprawl. These secluded spaces, shielded from the hustle of the streets, provide a haven for reflection and relaxation. Courtyards adorned with greenery, comfortable seating, and perhaps a small water feature become urban retreats that offer a break from the urban intensity.

Architectural Elements: Tranquility in Form and Function

The very form and function of architectural elements contribute to the creation of tranquil retreats. Designers employ principles of symmetry, balance, and simplicity to evoke a sense of calm. Functional elements, such as strategically placed benches, pergolas, and shading devices, are not merely utilitarian but are designed to enhance the overall tranquility of the space.

Seamless Indoor-Outdoor Transitions

Blurring the boundaries between indoor and outdoor spaces becomes a key strategy in creating urban retreats. Large windows, glass walls, and open-air designs allow natural light to flood interiors while providing seamless views of greenery and water features. The transition from the confined urban setting to an open, airy retreat becomes a sensory experience that enhances the overall sense of tranquility.

Wellness Architecture: Integrating Health and Design

The concept of wellness architecture takes center stage in the creation of urban retreats. Architects consciously integrate design elements that contribute to the physical and mental well-being of inhabitants. Biophilic design principles, natural materials, and considerations for air and light quality are woven into the fabric of urban retreats to create environments that support holistic health.

Art in Urban Retreats: Aesthetic Meditation

Art becomes a powerful medium for cultivating tranquility within urban retreats. Sculptures, murals, and installations not only serve as aesthetic focal points but also evoke contemplation and introspection. The strategic placement of art in urban retreats encourages inhabitants to engage with their surroundings on a deeper level, transcending the everyday urban experience.

Adaptable Spaces: From Quiet Contemplation to Social Connection

Urban retreats are designed to cater to diverse needs, providing spaces for solitary reflection as well as communal interactions. Adaptable seating arrangements, flexible use of space, and the incorporation of modular elements allow urban retreats to transform based on the preferences of their inhabitants. From quiet corners for reading to communal areas for socializing, these spaces become dynamic and responsive to the ebb and flow of urban life.

Technological Integration for Tranquility

In the era of smart cities, technological integration is not excluded from the creation of urban retreats. Architects explore innovative solutions such as smart lighting, soundscapes, and interactive installations to enhance the tranquil experience. Technology is harnessed to create immersive and responsive environments that adapt to the needs and preferences of urban inhabitants.

Community Engagement and Participation

The success of urban retreats hinges on community engagement and participation. Architects and urban planners involve the community in the design process, understanding the specific needs and desires of the people who will inhabit these spaces. This collaborative approach fosters a sense of ownership and ensures that urban retreats truly resonate with the cultural and social fabric of the community.

Challenges in Urban Retreat Design

Creating tranquil retreats within urban spaces is not without its challenges. Limited space, zoning restrictions, and the need for practical functionality pose considerations for architects. Overcoming these challenges involves creative problem-solving, innovative design solutions, and a commitment to the transformative power of tranquil urban retreats.

Summary

The chapter has explored the art and science of creating tranquil retreats within the vibrant tapestry of urban spaces. From the integration of greenery and water features to the thoughtful design of architectural elements and the seamless transition between indoor and outdoor spaces, architects are redefining urban living. As we navigate the evolving landscape of urban design, the journey continues towards crafting spaces that not only accommodate urban lifestyles but also provide moments of tranquility, connection, and rejuvenation.

Harmony in Color: Aesthetics and Emotional Well-being

In the palette of architectural design, color emerges as a powerful brushstroke, capable of evoking emotions, shaping perceptions, and influencing the overall well-being of occupants. This chapter delves into the intricate interplay of color in the built environment, exploring how thoughtful color choices and harmonious combinations contribute to aesthetics and emotional well-being.

The Psychology of Color

Color, beyond its visual appeal, has a profound impact on human psychology. The study of color psychology reveals that different hues can elicit specific emotional and physiological responses. Warm colors, such as reds and yellows, are often associated with energy and vibrancy, while cool colors, like blues and greens, evoke a sense of calm and tranquility. Understanding this interplay is crucial for architects seeking to create environments that resonate with the emotions and well-being of occupants.

Creating Atmospheres with Color

Architects wield color as a tool for crafting atmospheres within built spaces. The careful selection of a color palette sets the tone for the entire environment, influencing how people feel and behave within a given space. Whether it's a vibrant and lively atmosphere in a communal area or a serene and calming ambiance in a private retreat, the nuances of color contribute to the overall experience of the built environment.

Harmony and Balance in Color Schemes

The art of color in architecture extends beyond individual hues to encompass the harmony and balance achieved through well-crafted color schemes. Monochromatic schemes, analogous combinations, and complementary contrasts are just a few of the strategies architects use to create visual interest while maintaining a sense of cohesion. Achieving harmony in color schemes is a delicate dance that involves an understanding of color theory and a keen eye for balance.

Nature-Inspired Color Palettes

Drawing inspiration from the natural world, architects often turn to nature-inspired color palettes. Earthy tones, such as browns and greens, evoke a connection to the outdoors and a sense of grounding. The soft blues and grays of the sky and water bring a serene and calming influence. Nature-inspired color choices not only align with biophilic design principles but also contribute to a harmonious and visually pleasing environment.

Color Temperature: Warmth and Coolness

Color temperature, a characteristic associated with the perceived warmth or coolness of a color, plays a crucial role in creating emotional responses. Warm colors, like reds and yellows, are perceived as cozy and inviting, while cool colors, such as blues and greens, convey a sense of freshness and calm. Architects use color temperature strategically to evoke specific moods and enhance the overall atmosphere of a space.

Accent Colors: Focal Points and Emotional Highlights

In the symphony of color, accent hues function as focal points, directing attention and imbuing spaces with emotional highlights. Vibrant accent colors strategically placed within a neutral or subdued color palette draw the eye and create moments of visual interest. These accents contribute to the dynamic quality of a space, allowing architects to guide the occupant's focus and influence their emotional experience.

Cultural Significance of Color

Color carries cultural significance, and architects must be attuned to the cultural contexts of the spaces they design. In different cultures, colors can symbolize varying emotions, traditions, and beliefs. For example, red may symbolize luck and prosperity in some cultures, while it may signify caution or danger in others. Sensitivity to cultural meanings ensures that color choices resonate positively and respectfully with the diverse backgrounds of occupants.

Color in Spatial Perception: Size and Proportion

The strategic use of color can influence the perception of size and proportion within a space. Lighter colors tend to make spaces feel larger and more open, while darker hues create a sense of coziness and intimacy. Architects leverage this perceptual effect to enhance the functionality and mood of different areas within a building, creating spatial experiences that align with the intended purpose of each space.

Healthcare Environments: Healing Hues

In healthcare environments, the role of color takes on a special significance. Architects and designers choose colors that contribute to the healing process and the overall well-being of patients. Soft, soothing hues are often employed to create a calming and comfortable atmosphere. The use of nature-inspired colors, such as greens and blues, has been linked to stress reduction and a positive impact on the mental state of patients.

Workplace Dynamics: Productivity and Creativity

In the workplace, color becomes a strategic tool for influencing productivity and creativity. Warm tones may foster a sense of energy and collaboration in communal areas, while cool tones in individual workspaces contribute to focus and concentration. Architects consider the nature of the work conducted in different areas and tailor color choices to support the specific needs and dynamics of the workforce.

Residential Retreats: Personalized Color Experiences

In residential design, the personal nature of living spaces allows for more personalized color experiences. Homeowners often have distinct preferences and emotional connections to certain colors. Architects collaborate with residents to create interiors that reflect individual tastes, while also considering the psychological impact of color choices on the overall mood and well-being of the occupants.

Temporal Dynamics: The Influence of Time of Day

The interplay of natural and artificial lighting throughout the day introduces a temporal dimension to the use of color in architecture. Colors may appear different under various lighting conditions, influencing the overall mood of a space. Architects consider how colors will interact with changing light throughout the day, creating environments that adapt and maintain a harmonious atmosphere from dawn to dusk.

Color Trends and Innovations

The world of color in architecture is not static; it evolves with trends and innovations. Architects stay attuned to current color trends, exploring new palettes and combinations that resonate with contemporary sensibilities. Innovations in color technology, such as smart lighting systems that allow for dynamic color changes, provide architects with new tools to create immersive and adaptive color experiences.

Challenges and Considerations

While color is a powerful tool, architects also face challenges in its application. Personal preferences, cultural differences, and the potential for color to evoke unintended emotions require careful consideration. Achieving the desired emotional impact involves a nuanced understanding of the specific context, purpose, and cultural nuances surrounding each architectural project.

Summary

The chapter has unraveled the rich tapestry of color in architecture, exploring its psychological impact, the creation of harmonious color schemes, and its role in shaping emotional experiences within built environments. From the cultural significance of color to its influence on spatial perception, the art of employing color is a dynamic and multifaceted aspect of architectural design. As architects navigate the nuanced world of color, the journey continues towards creating spaces that not only please the eye but also resonate with the emotions and well-being of their occupants.

Acoustic Design for Serene Environments

In the intricate symphony of architectural design, the role of acoustics emerges as a conductor, shaping the auditory landscape of built environments. This chapter delves into the art and science of acoustic design, exploring how thoughtful consideration of sound and noise contributes to the creation of serene environments that foster tranquility, concentration, and overall well-being.

The Impact of Sound on Well-being

Sound, a pervasive element in our daily lives, has a profound impact on our well-being. Unwanted noise, whether from traffic, machinery, or other sources, can induce stress, disrupt concentration, and hinder relaxation. On the flip side, intentional soundscapes, such as gentle water features or soothing music, can enhance the overall ambiance of a space and contribute to a sense of tranquility. Acoustic design seeks to harness these principles, creating environments where the auditory experience aligns with the desired emotional and functional goals.

Understanding the Basics of Acoustics

Acoustics, the study of sound, encompasses a range of phenomena, from the propagation of sound waves to their absorption, reflection, and transmission within a space. Architects delve into the principles of acoustics to understand how sound interacts with different materials, surfaces, and spatial configurations. This knowledge forms the foundation for designing spaces that optimize the acoustic experience for their intended purposes.

Noise Control in Urban Environments

In urban environments, the challenge of noise control looms large. Architects grapple with mitigating the impact of external noise sources, such as traffic, construction, and other urban activities. Strategies include the use of sound barriers, acoustic glass, and the strategic placement of buildings and outdoor spaces to minimize the intrusion of unwanted noise. Noise control measures are crucial for creating serene environments in the midst of bustling urbanity.

Internal Acoustics: Shaping the Sound Within

Beyond external noise, architects address internal acoustics to shape the sound environment within a building. The design of spaces with different functions requires tailored acoustic solutions. For example, open office layouts may benefit from sound-absorbing materials to reduce reverberation, while auditoriums may require acoustic treatments to enhance clarity and projection. The goal is to create environments where the acoustics support the intended activities and contribute to a harmonious auditory experience.

Materials and Surfaces: Absorption and Reflection

The selection of materials and surfaces plays a pivotal role in acoustic design. Sound-absorbing materials, such as acoustic panels, ceiling baffles, and wall treatments, mitigate echoes and reduce reverberation. On the other hand, reflective surfaces can be strategically used to enhance the projection of sound in spaces where clarity and amplification are essential. The balance between absorption and reflection is finely tuned to achieve optimal acoustic performance.

Biophilic Acoustics: Nature-Inspired Soundscapes

Biophilic design principles extend to the auditory realm through the concept of biophilic acoustics. Inspired by nature, architects integrate soundscapes that mimic natural sounds, such as flowing water, rustling leaves, or birdsong. These intentional sounds not only mask unwanted noise but also evoke a connection to nature, contributing to a sense of tranquility and well-being. Biophilic acoustics align with the broader goal of creating environments that resonate with our innate affinity for the natural world.

Privacy and Confidentiality: Acoustic Separation

In spaces where privacy and confidentiality are paramount, acoustic design takes on a critical role. Confidential conversations in offices, medical facilities, or legal settings necessitate acoustic separation to prevent the inadvertent transmission of sound. Architects implement strategies such as soundproofing, double-glazed windows, and sound masking systems to ensure that sensitive information remains confidential and undisturbed.

Residential Sanctuaries: Acoustic Comfort at Home

In residential design, the concept of acoustic comfort becomes integral to creating sanctuaries where inhabitants can escape the noise of the outside world. Soundproofing measures, such as insulated walls and windows, help create peaceful interiors. Additionally, interior design elements, like rugs, curtains, and upholstered furniture, contribute to sound absorption, enhancing the overall acoustic comfort of residential spaces.

Concert Halls and Auditoriums: Precision in Acoustics

In venues dedicated to music and performance, such as concert halls and auditoriums, the precision of acoustics is of paramount importance. Architects collaborate with acousticians to design spaces that optimize sound reflection, diffraction, and absorption to create an immersive and high-fidelity auditory experience. The unique architectural features, such as the shape of the space and the materials used, are meticulously tailored to achieve the desired acoustic qualities.

Healthcare Environments: Healing Soundscapes

In healthcare settings, where the auditory environment can significantly impact patient well-being, architects employ acoustic design to create healing soundscapes. The integration of nature-inspired sounds, soothing music, and the reduction of intrusive noise contribute to an environment that supports the healing process. From patient rooms to waiting areas, the acoustics of healthcare spaces are curated to enhance comfort and reduce stress.

Educational Spaces: Acoustic Adaptability

Educational environments, from classrooms to lecture halls, require adaptable acoustics that cater to diverse learning activities. Architects design spaces with acoustic flexibility, incorporating features like sound-absorbing panels, moveable partitions, and advanced audio systems. The goal is to create environments where clarity of communication is ensured, whether during a lecture, group discussion, or individual study.

Technological Innovations in Acoustics

Advancements in technology bring innovative solutions to the field of acoustic design. Acoustic modeling software allows architects to simulate and analyze the acoustic performance of spaces before construction. Smart acoustics systems, equipped with sensors and adaptive technologies, enable real-time adjustments to optimize the auditory experience based on changing conditions. These technological innovations enhance the precision and efficiency of acoustic design.

Occupant Engagement in Acoustic Design

In the pursuit of creating serene environments, architects recognize the importance of occupant engagement in the acoustic design process. Understanding the preferences and needs of the end-users ensures that the acoustics align with the intended use and emotional experience of the space. Feedback mechanisms, surveys, and user studies become integral tools for architects seeking to create environments that resonate with the diverse auditory sensitivities of their occupants.

Challenges and Considerations

Acoustic design is not without its challenges. The multifaceted nature of sound, coupled with varying preferences and sensitivities among occupants, poses complexities. Striking the right balance between absorption and reflection, addressing the diversity of auditory experiences, and overcoming budget constraints are considerations that architects navigate in their quest to achieve optimal acoustic design.

Summary

In the orchestration of serene environments, acoustic design emerges as a vital conductor, shaping the auditory landscape of built spaces. This chapter has explored the impact of sound on well-being, the principles of acoustics, and the role of thoughtful design in creating environments that prioritize tranquility. From urban noise control to the precision of acoustics in concert halls, the journey into acoustic design continues, orchestrating spaces that not only please the ears but also contribute to the overall well-being of their inhabitants.

The Role of Feng Shui in Holistic Architecture

In the pursuit of holistic architecture, designers and architects are increasingly turning to ancient wisdom and practices that harmonize the built environment with natural forces. Among these practices, Feng Shui stands out as a profound and time-honored system that seeks to create spaces that promote balance, well-being, and positive energy flow. This chapter explores the rich tapestry of Feng Shui in holistic architecture, delving into its principles, applications, and the transformative impact it can have on the occupant's experience.

Foundations of Feng Shui

Originating from ancient Chinese philosophy, Feng Shui translates to "wind" and "water," symbolizing the flow of energy that animates the universe. At its core, Feng Shui is rooted in the belief that the arrangement of our surroundings profoundly affects the flow of energy, or "qi," and subsequently, our well-being. The practice seeks to create environments where the forces of nature and the built elements exist in harmonious balance.

Five Elements and Yin-Yang Harmony

Central to Feng Shui are the concepts of the five elements (wood, fire, earth, metal, and water) and the balance of Yin and Yang energies. Each element is associated with specific qualities and attributes, and their proper arrangement is believed to enhance energy flow and create a harmonious environment. Balancing the opposing forces of Yin (passive) and Yang (active) energies is integral to achieving equilibrium in a space.

Bagua: The Energy Map

Feng Shui employs the Bagua, an octagonal energy map, as a tool for analyzing the energy distribution within a space. The Bagua divides a space into nine zones, each corresponding to different aspects of life, such as wealth, health, career, and relationships. By aligning the Bagua with the layout of a building or room, architects can strategically enhance specific areas to promote positive energy and support the holistic well-being of occupants.

Optimal Site Selection

In holistic architecture, the site selection of a building is of paramount importance, and Feng Shui offers insights into optimizing this process. The natural features surrounding a site, including landforms, water bodies, and vegetation, are considered in relation to the principles of energy flow. Proper orientation, alignment, and placement of buildings on a site are believed to influence the flow of qi, fostering a connection with the Earth's energies.

Building Design and Layout

Feng Shui principles extend to the design and layout of buildings. Architects consider factors such as the flow of energy through entrances, the placement of rooms, and the use of natural light. The aim is to create spaces that not only align with the Bagua but also enhance the occupant's experience and support their activities. Thoughtful design choices, such as avoiding sharp angles and incorporating natural materials, contribute to a sense of balance and positive energy.

Flow of Qi: Open Spaces and Circulation

The concept of qi emphasizes the importance of unobstructed energy flow throughout a space. Architects integrate open layouts and well-designed circulation paths to facilitate the smooth movement of energy. Avoiding clutter and ensuring that furniture and architectural elements do not impede the flow of qi are key considerations in Feng Shui. This approach creates spaces that feel spacious, inviting, and energetically balanced.

Natural Elements in Design

Incorporating natural elements into the built environment is a fundamental tenet of holistic architecture influenced by Feng Shui. The use of materials such as wood, stone, and water features connects the built environment with nature, enhancing the flow of positive energy. Living elements, such as indoor plants, contribute not only to aesthetics but also to a vibrant and healthful energy within the space.

Color and Symbolism

Color plays a significant role in Feng Shui, with each color associated with specific elements and energies. Architects carefully select color schemes that align with the Bagua and promote the desired qualities in different areas of a building. Additionally, symbolism is considered in design choices, with certain objects and motifs believed to carry positive energy and enhance the overall harmonious atmosphere.

Sacred Geometry and Proportions

The principles of sacred geometry and proportional harmony are integrated into Feng Shui-influenced architecture. Certain proportions, such as the Golden Ratio, are believed to resonate with natural harmony and create spaces that feel balanced and aesthetically pleasing. Architects may incorporate these proportions into building layouts, room dimensions, and architectural details to enhance the overall sense of equilibrium.

Enhancing Specific Aspects of Life

One of the distinctive features of Feng Shui is its ability to address specific aspects of life by enhancing corresponding areas within a space. For example, to promote wealth and prosperity, architects may focus on the southeast area of a building, incorporating elements associated with abundance and growth. Similarly, the northeast area might be emphasized for career advancement, and the southwest for relationships. This tailored approach allows architects to align the design with the unique needs and aspirations of the occupants.

Residential Applications: Creating Harmonious Homes

In residential architecture, the principles of Feng Shui are often applied to create homes that nurture well-being and harmony. Architects work closely with homeowners to understand their goals and aspirations, using the Bagua to optimize the layout, design, and energy flow within the home. This personalized approach results in residences that not only meet functional needs but also support the holistic lifestyle and aspirations of the occupants.

Commercial and Public Spaces

Feng Shui is also integrated into the design of commercial and public spaces to create environments that foster positive energy and support the well-being of occupants. From offices to shopping centers and public institutions, architects apply Feng Shui principles to enhance the flow of energy, create harmonious layouts, and promote positive experiences for employees, customers, and visitors.

The Mind-Body Connection

Holistic architecture, influenced by Feng Shui, recognizes the interconnectedness of the mind and body with the built environment. A space that aligns with the principles of positive energy flow is believed to contribute to physical health, mental well-being, and overall harmony. Architects, therefore, play a pivotal role in shaping environments that not only serve practical functions but also nurture the holistic health of the individuals who inhabit them.

Challenges and Integration

While the principles of Feng Shui offer valuable insights, integrating them into contemporary architectural practices presents challenges. Balancing ancient wisdom with modern design requirements, addressing diverse cultural contexts, and navigating varying interpretations of Feng Shui principles require a nuanced approach. Architects must carefully consider how to incorporate these principles in ways that align with the project's goals and the needs of the occupants.

Summary

The role of Feng Shui in holistic architecture is a captivating journey into the ancient wisdom that seeks to harmonize the built environment with natural energies. From site selection to building design, color choices, and the arrangement of spaces, Feng Shui principles offer a holistic approach to architecture that goes beyond aesthetics. As architects continue to explore the integration of ancient practices with contemporary design, the quest for spaces that inspire balance, well-being, and positive energy unfolds, creating environments that resonate with the human spirit.

Wellness-Centric Furniture and Interior Elements

In the realm of holistic architecture and interior design, the concept of wellness takes center stage as an overarching goal. As the awareness of the profound impact of built environments on physical and mental well-being grows, designers are increasingly turning their attention to creating spaces that prioritize health and harmony. This chapter explores the realm of wellness-centric furniture and interior elements, delving into innovative designs, mindful material choices, and the transformative influence these elements can have on the overall well-being of occupants.

Ergonomics: Designing for Human Well-being

At the core of wellness-centric furniture lies the principle of ergonomics – the study of designing products and environments that are tailored to the human body's natural movements and capabilities. Ergonomic furniture aims to optimize comfort, support, and efficiency, reducing the risk of musculoskeletal disorders and enhancing overall well-being. Adjustable chairs, sit-stand desks, and customized seating solutions are examples of how ergonomics is integrated into modern interiors to create spaces that promote physical health.

Biophilic Design in Furniture

Biophilic design, inspired by the innate human connection to nature, is a cornerstone of wellness-centric interiors. Furniture that incorporates natural materials, textures, and organic forms brings the outdoors inside, fostering a sense of connection with the environment. Wooden furnishings, stone accents, and plant-inspired shapes not only contribute to aesthetics but also evoke a calming and grounding atmosphere within the space.

Adaptable and Modular Furniture

The dynamic nature of modern living requires furniture that adapts to diverse needs and functions. Adaptable and modular furniture designs address this demand by offering flexibility and versatility. From modular seating arrangements that can be rearranged to suit different activities to furniture with hidden storage solutions, these designs contribute to creating dynamic and functional spaces that cater to the evolving needs of occupants.

Sensory Furniture: Tactile and Textural Experiences

Wellness-centric interiors go beyond visual appeal, engaging the senses to create a holistic experience. Sensory furniture focuses on tactile and textural elements, providing occupants with a range of touch-based experiences. Soft, plush fabrics, smooth wooden surfaces, and textured materials not only enhance the aesthetics of furniture but also invite touch, contributing to a sensory-rich environment that elevates the overall well-being of individuals.

Color Psychology in Furniture Design

The influence of color on emotions and mood is a well-established principle, and furniture designers leverage this knowledge to create wellness-centric interiors. Color psychology is applied to furniture design by selecting hues that evoke specific feelings and contribute to the desired atmosphere. Calming blues, invigorating greens, and warm neutrals are strategically incorporated into furniture pieces, influencing the emotional experience of the space.

Lighting as a Wellness Element

Lighting is a pivotal element in wellness-centric interiors, and furniture plays a role in optimizing the effects of light. Furniture designs may incorporate features such as integrated lighting, adjustable fixtures, or materials that enhance natural light diffusion. By considering the interaction between furniture and lighting, designers create interiors that support circadian rhythms, reduce eye strain, and contribute to a sense of well-being.

Innovative Seating Solutions

The sedentary nature of many modern lifestyles has led to a focus on innovative seating solutions that prioritize both comfort and health. Ergonomic chairs with lumbar support, balance ball chairs that engage core muscles, and active sitting options like standing desks promote movement and contribute to better posture. These seating solutions acknowledge the importance of physical activity and aim to counteract the negative effects of prolonged sitting.

Holistic Bedrooms: Wellness in Sleep Spaces

The bedroom, a sanctuary for rest and rejuvenation, is a key focus of wellness-centric interior design. Furniture in bedrooms is curated to enhance sleep quality and overall well-being. Comfortable mattresses, supportive pillows, and breathable bedding materials contribute to creating a sleep environment that promotes relaxation and restful sleep. The arrangement of furniture in bedrooms is mindful of creating a harmonious atmosphere conducive to restorative rest.

Mindful Living Room Design

In the living room, where families gather and individuals unwind, wellness-centric furniture plays a crucial role in creating spaces that foster connection and relaxation. Comfortable and inviting seating arrangements, adaptable furniture configurations, and the integration of natural elements contribute to a living room environment that supports social interaction and mental well-being.

Spa-Inspired Bathrooms: Furniture and Tranquility

Bathrooms, often overlooked in terms of wellness design, are gaining prominence as spaces for relaxation and self-care. Furniture in spa-inspired bathrooms goes beyond mere functionality, incorporating elements that contribute to tranquility. Freestanding soaking tubs, comfortable seating, and vanity designs that prioritize both aesthetics and functionality create a spa-like atmosphere that enhances the overall wellness experience.

Wellness in Workplace Design

As the concept of wellness extends to the workplace, furniture and interior elements play a pivotal role in creating office environments that prioritize the health and productivity of employees. Ergonomic office chairs, sit-stand desks, collaborative seating arrangements, and biophilic design elements contribute to workplaces that support physical health, mental well-being, and a positive work culture.

Green Building Materials: Sustainable Wellness

The materials used in furniture and interior design have a direct impact on the well-being of both occupants and the planet. Wellness-centric interiors prioritize the use of sustainable, non-toxic materials that contribute to indoor air quality. Furniture made from recycled or upcycled materials, low-VOC finishes, and responsibly sourced wood align with the principles of holistic architecture, promoting both personal and environmental health.

Technological Integration for Wellness

In the era of smart homes and workplaces, technological integration in furniture design enhances the wellness-centric experience. Smart furniture may include features such as built-in air purifiers, adjustable settings for lighting and temperature, and even monitoring systems that provide feedback on posture and ergonomic habits. These technological innovations contribute to creating intelligent and responsive interiors that cater to the well-being of occupants.

Multisensory Environments

Wellness-centric interiors aim to engage multiple senses to create enriching environments. Multisensory furniture designs incorporate elements that appeal to sight, touch, sound, and even scent. Aromatherapy diffusers, sound-enhancing furniture, and visually stimulating designs contribute to a holistic sensory experience, promoting relaxation, focus, and overall well-being.

Community and Connection in Interior Design

Wellness-centric interior design extends beyond individual spaces to consider the impact on community and social well-being. Furniture arrangements that encourage social interaction, communal spaces designed for connection, and shared elements that foster a sense of belonging contribute to a holistic approach that recognizes the importance of community in overall wellness.

Challenges in Implementing Wellness-Centric Design

Despite the growing enthusiasm for wellness-centric design, challenges exist in its widespread implementation. Cost considerations, conflicting design preferences, and the need for education and awareness present hurdles for designers and occupants alike. Overcoming these challenges requires a collaborative approach, where designers, manufacturers, and occupants work together to prioritize wellness in the built environment.

Summary

Wellness-centric furniture and interior elements represent a transformative approach to architectural and design practices. From ergonomic solutions that prioritize physical health to sensory-rich environments that enhance mental well-being, these elements contribute to creating spaces that prioritize holistic wellness. As designers continue to explore innovative concepts, integrate technological advancements, and prioritize sustainability, the journey toward wellness-centric interiors unfolds, promising spaces that resonate with the diverse well-being needs of their occupants.

Innovative Technologies for Healthy Living Spaces

In the rapidly evolving landscape of architecture and design, innovative technologies are playing a pivotal role in reshaping living spaces to prioritize health and well-being. This chapter explores cutting-edge technologies that contribute to the creation of healthy living environments, addressing aspects ranging from air and water quality to smart home integrations and advanced building materials.

Smart Home Automation for Health

The advent of smart home technologies has ushered in a new era of convenience and control, and these innovations are now being harnessed to enhance health in living spaces. Smart home automation systems allow residents to monitor and control various aspects of their home environment, from lighting and temperature to security and air quality. Integration with voice-activated assistants and mobile devices enables users to create personalized, health-focused settings that adapt to their preferences and routines.

Air Purification Systems

Indoor air quality is a critical factor in promoting a healthy living environment. Innovative air purification systems equipped with advanced filters and sensors are becoming integral components of modern homes. These systems can efficiently remove pollutants, allergens, and airborne particles, contributing to respiratory health and overall well-being. Some systems are designed to be seamlessly integrated into HVAC systems, ensuring comprehensive air purification throughout the entire living space.

HVAC Technologies for Efficient Ventilation

Heating, ventilation, and air conditioning (HVAC) systems have undergone significant advancements to improve both energy efficiency and indoor air quality. Innovations include energy recovery ventilators that exchange stale indoor air with fresh outdoor air while retaining the desired temperature. Additionally, smart HVAC systems can adapt to occupancy patterns and outdoor air quality, optimizing ventilation for a healthier living environment.

Water Purification and Filtration Systems

Access to clean and safe water is fundamental to well-being, and innovative water purification systems are addressing this need within living spaces. Advanced filtration technologies, such as reverse osmosis and UV purification, remove impurities, contaminants, and bacteria from tap water. Some systems can be integrated directly into kitchen faucets or installed at the point of entry to ensure that every water source in the home delivers high-quality, potable water.

Biophilic Design and Nature-Infused Technologies

Biophilic design principles, which emphasize the integration of nature into the built environment, are being enhanced through technology. Nature-infused technologies bring elements of the outdoors inside, fostering a connection with the natural world. Digital displays that mimic natural scenes, smart windows that adjust transparency based on outdoor conditions, and even virtual reality experiences that simulate natural environments contribute to a sense of well-being and tranquility.

Lighting Systems for Circadian Health

The impact of lighting on circadian rhythms and overall health is well-established, and innovative lighting systems are being designed to support these natural cycles. Human-centric lighting mimics the color temperature and intensity of natural sunlight throughout the day, promoting alertness in the morning and a gradual transition to warmer tones in the evening to support relaxation and sleep. Smart lighting controls allow users to personalize their lighting environments based on daily routines and preferences.

Healthy Building Materials

The choice of building materials has a direct impact on indoor air quality, and innovative materials are emerging to address this concern. Low-VOC (volatile organic compound) paints and finishes, formaldehyde-free adhesives, and sustainable, non-toxic materials contribute to healthier indoor environments. Some materials are designed to actively improve air quality by absorbing pollutants or releasing beneficial ions, further enhancing the well-being of occupants.

Wellness Apps and Monitoring Devices

The proliferation of wellness apps and monitoring devices is empowering individuals to take an active role in managing their health within the home. From fitness trackers that monitor physical activity to apps that provide guided meditation sessions and sleep tracking devices that optimize bedroom environments for restful sleep, these technologies contribute to a holistic approach to well-being within the living space.

Smart Furniture and Ergonomics

The integration of smart technologies extends to furniture, with innovative designs incorporating sensors, actuators, and connectivity features. Smart furniture may include adjustable desks that encourage movement throughout the day, chairs with built-in posture monitoring, and even beds that adapt to individual sleep preferences. These technologies aim to enhance comfort, support, and overall physical well-being.

Robotic Cleaners and Maintenance

Automation is increasingly becoming a valuable ally in maintaining a clean and healthy living space. Robotic vacuum cleaners equipped with advanced sensors navigate through homes, efficiently removing dust and allergens from floors. Similarly, robotic window cleaners and air duct cleaning robots contribute to maintaining a hygienic indoor environment, reducing the need for manual labor and ensuring consistent cleanliness.

Privacy and Security Considerations

As technology becomes more integrated into living spaces, considerations for privacy and security are paramount. Homeowners and designers must balance the benefits of innovative technologies with the need to protect personal data and maintain a secure living environment. Encrypted communication protocols, secure network configurations, and user-friendly privacy settings are essential features to ensure the responsible implementation of these technologies.

Energy-Efficient Home Systems

Sustainability and energy efficiency are integral aspects of healthy living spaces. Innovative technologies in energy management systems, solar panels, and home automation contribute to reducing energy consumption and environmental impact. Smart thermostats that optimize heating and cooling based on occupancy, energy-efficient appliances, and home energy monitoring systems empower residents to make eco-conscious choices.

Personalized Climate Control

Innovative climate control technologies are enabling personalized comfort within living spaces. Smart HVAC systems with room-level temperature sensors allow for individualized climate preferences in different areas of the home. Personalized climate control not only enhances comfort but also supports well-being by addressing individual thermal comfort needs.

Challenges and Considerations

The integration of innovative technologies into living spaces brings forth challenges that must be carefully navigated. These include the potential for data breaches and privacy concerns, the need for standardized communication protocols, and the challenge of ensuring accessibility and usability for users of all ages and abilities. Additionally, the rapid pace of technological advancements necessitates thoughtful planning to future-proof homes and prevent obsolescence.

Summary

Innovative technologies are transforming living spaces into dynamic environments that prioritize health and well-being. From air and water purification to smart home automation, these technologies contribute to creating homes that actively support the physical, mental, and emotional wellness of their occupants. As designers and homeowners continue to embrace these advancements, the journey towards healthier living spaces evolves, promising a future where technology seamlessly integrates with the fundamental elements that contribute to a holistic sense of well-being.

Adaptive Reuse: Transforming Spaces for Well-being

In the pursuit of sustainable and people-centric urban development, the concept of adaptive reuse has emerged as a transformative approach to architecture. This chapter explores how adaptive reuse, the process of repurposing existing structures for new functionalities, contributes to the creation of spaces that prioritize well-being. From historical landmarks to industrial sites, the adaptive reuse movement embodies the principles of sustainability, community engagement, and holistic design.

Preserving Heritage, Promoting Wellness

Adaptive reuse breathes new life into existing structures, preserving the rich tapestry of architectural heritage while addressing contemporary needs. Historical buildings, once facing the threat of decay or demolition, are revitalized to serve as vibrant spaces that contribute to the well-being of their communities. The process involves retaining key architectural elements, respecting the cultural significance of the original structure, and integrating modern design principles to enhance functionality.

Transforming Industrial Spaces into Wellness Hubs

One remarkable facet of adaptive reuse is its ability to repurpose industrial spaces into wellness-centric environments. Abandoned factories, warehouses, and mills are given a new lease on life as fitness centers, art studios, or community hubs. The inherent character of these industrial structures, with their lofty ceilings and expansive spaces, provides a unique canvas for architects to create environments that inspire physical activity, creativity, and community engagement.

The Adaptive Reuse Process: Balancing Preservation and Innovation

Successful adaptive reuse projects strike a delicate balance between preserving the historical integrity of a structure and introducing innovative design solutions. Architects engage in extensive research to understand the historical context, architectural significance, and structural integrity of the existing building. Through a collaborative process involving preservation experts, designers, and community stakeholders, the adaptive reuse project takes shape, respecting the past while embracing the future.

Community-Centric Spaces: Fostering Social Well-being

Adaptive reuse projects often become community hubs that foster social well-being. Repurposed structures, whether old schools, churches, or warehouses, serve as gathering places where people can connect, collaborate, and engage in shared activities. The communal aspect of adaptive reuse contributes to a sense of belonging and social cohesion, addressing the inherent human need for community and positively impacting the mental and emotional well-being of residents.

Historic Landmarks as Wellness Destinations

Transforming historic landmarks into wellness destinations is a testament to the versatility of adaptive reuse. Old libraries become vibrant cultural centers, offering spaces for art exhibitions, workshops, and community events. Former theaters are reborn as fitness studios, weaving together the charm of the past with the energy of contemporary activities. These adaptive reuse projects not only preserve architectural treasures but also contribute to the cultural vitality and well-being of the community.

Repurposing Educational Institutions: Learning and Well-being

Educational institutions, with their unique architectural character, are prime candidates for adaptive reuse. Old school buildings, universities, or libraries find new life as innovative learning spaces, co-working offices, or cultural centers. The adaptive reuse of educational structures reflects a commitment to lifelong learning and intellectual well-being, providing spaces that inspire creativity, collaboration, and the pursuit of knowledge.

Adaptive Reuse in Urban Planning: Sustainable Development

Adaptive reuse aligns seamlessly with the principles of sustainable urban development. By repurposing existing structures, cities reduce the environmental impact associated with new construction. This sustainable approach minimizes waste, conserves resources, and mitigates the ecological footprint of urban expansion. Adaptive reuse projects contribute to the creation of more walkable, livable urban spaces that prioritize environmental stewardship and the well-being of city dwellers.

Health and Wellness Facilities in Repurposed Structures

The adaptive reuse of structures for health and wellness facilities underscores the interconnectedness of physical spaces and well-being. Former factories and warehouses, with their spacious interiors and unique architectural features, are transformed into gyms, yoga studios, and wellness retreats. The adaptive reuse process allows designers to infuse these spaces with natural light, greenery, and thoughtful design elements that contribute to a holistic approach to health.

Biophilic Design in Adaptive Reuse

Biophilic design, which emphasizes the integration of nature into the built environment, finds a natural home in adaptive reuse projects. Repurposed structures often incorporate elements such as indoor gardens, green roofs, and natural materials, creating spaces that resonate with the human connection to nature. The biophilic features introduced during the adaptive reuse process contribute to improved air quality, reduced stress levels, and an overall sense of well-being.

Residential Adaptive Reuse: Homes with Character and History

Adaptive reuse extends its transformative influence to residential spaces, offering individuals the opportunity to live in homes with character, history, and a unique sense of place. Old warehouses become spacious loft apartments, and historic homes are repurposed to accommodate modern living needs while preserving their architectural charm. The result is a blend of old and new, where residents can experience the comfort and well-being associated with living in a thoughtfully repurposed home.

The Role of Technology in Adaptive Reuse

Technology plays a pivotal role in the adaptive reuse process, facilitating the integration of modern amenities while preserving the historical essence of a structure. 3D scanning and modeling assist architects in understanding the existing conditions of a building, enabling precise design interventions. Building information modeling (BIM) ensures that the adaptive reuse project is executed efficiently, with a focus on sustainability and well-being.

Challenges and Considerations in Adaptive Reuse

Despite its many benefits, adaptive reuse is not without its challenges. Preserving historical structures requires careful consideration of building codes, structural integrity, and accessibility standards. Striking a balance between innovation and preservation can be complex, as architects navigate the need for modern amenities without compromising the authenticity of the original structure. Additionally, community engagement and stakeholder involvement are critical for the success of adaptive reuse projects, as they often involve a collective vision for the future of a space.

Summary

Adaptive reuse stands at the intersection of history, sustainability, and well-being, offering a transformative approach to urban development. From repurposing industrial spaces into wellness hubs to preserving historic landmarks as vibrant cultural centers, adaptive reuse projects contribute to the creation of living environments that prioritize the physical, social, and cultural well-being of their occupants. As architects and communities continue to embrace the principles of adaptive reuse, the journey towards sustainable, people-centric spaces unfolds, promising a future where the past and present coexist in harmony for the benefit of well-being.

Holistic Approaches to Urban Planning

Urbanization is an undeniable global phenomenon, and as cities continue to evolve, the need for holistic approaches to urban planning becomes increasingly evident. This chapter explores the multifaceted strategies and philosophies that underpin holistic urban planning. From sustainable development and community engagement to green spaces and smart technologies, these approaches seek to create cities that prioritize the well-being of their residents while fostering environmental resilience and social equity.

Understanding Holistic Urban Planning

Holistic urban planning goes beyond traditional city development models by integrating diverse factors into the planning process. It acknowledges the interconnectedness of various elements, including environmental sustainability, social cohesion, economic vitality, and public health. Rather than viewing these aspects in isolation, holistic approaches seek to create a harmonious balance that enhances the overall well-being of urban dwellers.

Sustainable Development and Resilience

At the core of holistic urban planning is the commitment to sustainable development. This involves balancing urban growth with environmental preservation, resource efficiency, and the mitigation of climate change impacts. Sustainable cities prioritize green infrastructure, renewable energy sources, and eco-friendly transportation systems. Additionally, resilience planning considers the city's ability to withstand and recover from environmental challenges, such as extreme weather events or pandemics, ensuring the long-term well-being of its residents.

Community-Centered Design

Holistic urban planning places a strong emphasis on community engagement and participation. It recognizes that residents are the heart of any city and that their insights, needs, and aspirations should guide the planning process. Community-centered design involves collaborative workshops, public forums, and participatory decision-making, empowering residents to actively contribute to shaping their urban environment. This approach fosters a sense of ownership and strengthens social bonds, ultimately contributing to the well-being of individuals and communities.

Green Spaces and Biodiversity

The integration of green spaces within urban landscapes is a hallmark of holistic urban planning. Parks, gardens, and natural reserves contribute to the physical and mental well-being of city dwellers. Access to green spaces provides opportunities for recreation, relaxation, and connection with nature, fostering a healthier and more balanced urban lifestyle. Moreover, incorporating biodiversity into urban planning promotes ecological resilience, enhances air and water quality, and contributes to overall environmental sustainability.

Smart Technologies for Efficiency

Advancements in technology offer innovative solutions for enhancing the efficiency and well-being of urban spaces. Smart cities leverage data, sensors, and connectivity to optimize various aspects of urban life, from transportation and energy management to public safety and waste reduction. By embracing smart technologies, holistic urban planning aims to create cities that are not only more sustainable and efficient but also responsive to the evolving needs of their residents.

Mixed-Use Zoning and Walkability

Holistic urban planning often advocates for mixed-use zoning, where residential, commercial, and recreational spaces coexist within neighborhoods. This approach minimizes the need for long commutes, reduces traffic congestion, and creates vibrant, walkable communities. Walkable neighborhoods contribute to the physical well-being of residents by promoting active lifestyles, reducing reliance on cars, and fostering a sense of community connectivity.

Affordable Housing and Inclusive Development

Inclusivity is a fundamental principle of holistic urban planning, and this extends to housing. Creating affordable housing options within city centers ensures that diverse socioeconomic groups can access the benefits of urban living. Inclusive development strategies address the challenges of gentrification, displacement, and social inequality, striving to create cities where opportunities are accessible to all residents, regardless of their economic status.

Cultural Preservation and Identity

Preserving the cultural heritage and identity of urban areas is integral to holistic planning. Historical buildings, landmarks, and cultural institutions contribute to the unique character of a city. Holistic urban planning strategies seek to balance modernization with the preservation of cultural assets, fostering a sense of continuity and pride among residents. Celebrating diversity and supporting cultural expressions enrich the urban experience, contributing to the well-being of the community.

Public Transportation and Accessibility

Efficient and accessible transportation systems are key components of holistic urban planning. Public transportation infrastructure, such as buses, trains, and bike lanes, reduces traffic congestion, air pollution, and the overall environmental impact of commuting. Accessible transportation networks also promote social inclusion by ensuring that all residents, regardless of mobility constraints, can navigate the city easily, fostering an equitable and connected urban environment.

Social Services and Healthcare Accessibility

Holistic urban planning recognizes the importance of accessible social services and healthcare facilities. Strategically locating community centers, schools, and healthcare clinics within neighborhoods ensures that residents have easy access to essential services. This approach contributes to the physical and mental well-being of urban populations, reducing disparities in healthcare access and promoting community resilience.

Balancing Economic Development with Social Equity

Economic development is an essential component of urban planning, but holistic approaches seek to balance economic growth with social equity. This involves creating opportunities for local businesses, promoting job creation, and addressing income inequality. By fostering an inclusive economy, holistic urban planning aims to enhance the overall well-being of residents and create cities where prosperity is shared by diverse communities.

Challenges and Considerations

While holistic urban planning holds great promise, it comes with its share of challenges. Balancing competing interests, navigating political complexities, and securing funding for long-term projects can be daunting. Additionally, the dynamic nature of urban environments requires flexibility and adaptability in planning strategies. Overcoming these challenges demands collaboration among policymakers, urban planners, community members, and other stakeholders committed to the well-being of the city and its residents.

Summary

Holistic urban planning represents a paradigm shift in how cities are conceived, developed, and experienced. By embracing sustainability, community engagement, and a multifaceted understanding of well-being, holistic approaches aim to create cities that are not just functional but thriving hubs of vitality, inclusivity, and resilience. As urban areas continue to evolve, the principles of holistic urban planning offer a roadmap for creating environments that prioritize the well-being of current and future generations, fostering a harmonious relationship between people, communities, and their urban surroundings.

Community-Centered Design for Social Well-being

In the dynamic landscape of urban development, the concept of community-centered design has emerged as a transformative approach that places people and their well-being at the forefront of the planning process. This chapter delves into the principles and practices of community-centered design, exploring how it fosters social well-being, strengthens community bonds, and creates urban environments that resonate with the diverse needs and aspirations of their residents.

Understanding Community-Centered Design

At its core, community-centered design is a philosophy that prioritizes the active involvement of community members in shaping the spaces they inhabit. It goes beyond traditional top-down planning models, recognizing that the people who live, work, and play in a community possess valuable insights and perspectives. Community-centered design is a collaborative process that seeks to empower residents, create inclusive spaces, and address the unique challenges and opportunities of each neighborhood.

Empowering Communities through Participation

Central to community-centered design is the belief that residents are experts in their own experiences and needs. Through participatory methods, such as community workshops, charrettes, and collaborative decision-making processes, community members actively contribute to the design and development of their neighborhoods. This empowerment not only enhances the physical aspects of the built environment but also strengthens the social fabric, fostering a sense of ownership and pride among residents.

Placemaking: Crafting Spaces with Identity

A key aspect of community-centered design is the concept of placemaking, which involves creating spaces that reflect the identity and aspirations of the community. This goes beyond the functional aspects of architecture and planning to embrace the cultural, historical, and social narratives that define a place. Placemaking fosters a sense of belonging and connection, turning public spaces into vibrant hubs that celebrate the uniqueness of each community and contribute to social well-being.

Inclusive Design for Diversity

Community-centered design places a strong emphasis on inclusivity, recognizing the diversity of residents in terms of age, ability, socioeconomic status, and cultural backgrounds. Inclusive design principles ensure that spaces are accessible to all, promoting social equity and reducing barriers to participation. Features such as universally accessible infrastructure, multigenerational amenities, and cultural inclusivity contribute to creating environments that cater to the diverse needs of community members.

Building Social Infrastructure

Beyond physical structures, community-centered design prioritizes the creation of social infrastructure—spaces and programs that facilitate social interactions, foster relationships, and build a sense of community. This may include community centers, public gathering spaces, and programs that encourage communal activities. By investing in social infrastructure, community-centered design recognizes the importance of social connections in promoting mental and emotional well-being.

Community-Centered Housing: From Homes to Neighborhoods

Housing is a fundamental aspect of community well-being, and community-centered design extends its principles to residential areas. This involves not only designing homes that are comfortable and functional but also creating neighborhoods that encourage social interactions. Walkable streets, communal green spaces, and shared amenities contribute to a sense of community within residential areas, fostering social bonds and a supportive neighborhood environment.

Responsive to Cultural Context

Each community has its own cultural context, shaped by traditions, customs, and shared histories. Community-centered design is inherently responsive to this cultural context, seeking to integrate cultural elements into the built environment. This may involve incorporating public art, cultural markers, or architectural styles that reflect the heritage of the community. By respecting and celebrating cultural diversity, community-centered design contributes to a sense of pride and identity among residents.

Adaptive Reuse and Community Revitalization

Community-centered design often embraces adaptive reuse as a strategy for revitalizing neighborhoods. The repurposing of existing structures aligns with the principles of sustainability and preservation of community character. Adaptive reuse projects, guided by community input, can transform vacant buildings into vibrant hubs that meet the specific needs of residents, whether through community centers, co-working spaces, or cultural institutions.

Enhancing Public Safety and Security

A community-centered approach recognizes the importance of public safety in fostering social well-being. Designing spaces with visibility, well-lit areas, and clear wayfinding contributes to a sense of security. Involving residents in the planning process ensures that their concerns and perspectives regarding safety are integrated into the design, creating environments where residents feel safe and supported.

Promoting Active Transportation and Connectivity

Community-centered design encourages active transportation options, such as walking and cycling, to promote both physical health and community interactions. Creating pedestrian-friendly streets, bike lanes, and interconnected pathways enhances connectivity within neighborhoods. By prioritizing these elements, community-centered design contributes to reducing reliance on cars, minimizing traffic congestion, and creating environments that encourage outdoor activities and social encounters.

Education and Awareness Initiatives

Empowering communities through education and awareness initiatives is a key component of community-centered design. Informing residents about the design process, urban planning principles, and the potential impact of their involvement fosters a sense of civic responsibility. Workshops, seminars, and educational programs create opportunities for residents to build their capacity to actively engage in shaping the future of their communities.

Measuring Success through Resident Well-being

Community-centered design recognizes that the ultimate measure of success is the well-being of residents. This goes beyond traditional metrics of urban development and includes indicators such as social connectedness, mental health, and overall satisfaction with the living environment. By prioritizing resident well-being, community-centered design aims to create environments that enhance the quality of life for individuals and foster a strong sense of community.

Challenges and Considerations

While community-centered design offers promising benefits, it comes with its own set of challenges. Balancing diverse opinions and managing conflicting interests within a community can be complex. Additionally, ensuring that the design process is truly inclusive and representative of all voices requires ongoing effort and commitment. Navigating bureaucratic processes and securing resources for community-led initiatives can pose further challenges. Overcoming these hurdles demands collaboration, flexibility, and a commitment to the principles of inclusivity and equity.

Summary

Community-centered design stands as a powerful framework for creating urban environments that prioritize the social well-being of residents. By empowering communities, fostering inclusivity, and creating spaces that reflect the unique identity of each neighborhood, this approach goes beyond the traditional notions of urban planning. As cities continue to evolve, community-centered design offers a pathway to creating vibrant, resilient, and socially connected communities, where the well-being of individuals is at the heart of the urban experience.

Inclusive Design: Spaces for All Abilities

In the realm of urban development and architecture, the concept of inclusive design has emerged as a transformative approach that seeks to create spaces accessible and welcoming to individuals of all abilities. This chapter explores the principles, practices, and impact of inclusive design, delving into how it goes beyond mere compliance with accessibility standards to foster environments that celebrate diversity, promote equality, and enhance the overall well-being of communities.

Understanding Inclusive Design

Inclusive design, also known as universal design, is a philosophy that revolves around creating environments, products, and systems that are accessible and usable by people of all abilities, ages, and backgrounds. It goes beyond traditional accessibility measures, emphasizing a proactive and holistic approach that considers the diverse needs and experiences of users. The goal of inclusive design is to ensure that everyone, regardless of their abilities or disabilities, can participate fully and independently in all aspects of life.

Physical Accessibility: Beyond Compliance

While physical accessibility is a fundamental aspect of inclusive design, the philosophy goes beyond mere compliance with building codes and standards. Inclusive design seeks to create environments that are not only accessible but also intuitive and seamlessly integrated. This involves considering the needs of individuals with mobility challenges, visual or hearing impairments, and cognitive differences from the initial stages of design. Ramps, elevators, and accessible restrooms are essential elements, but inclusive design extends to features like tactile signage, audible signals, and universally designed furniture to enhance the overall user experience.

Flexible and Adaptable Spaces

Inclusive design embraces the idea of flexibility and adaptability within spaces. Recognizing that individuals have diverse preferences and needs, inclusive environments provide options that cater to different abilities and preferences. For instance, flexible seating arrangements in public spaces accommodate various body sizes and mobility devices, ensuring that everyone can find a comfortable and inclusive spot. The adaptability of spaces contributes to a sense of autonomy and empowerment for users.

Cognitive Accessibility: Beyond Physical Barriers

Inclusive design extends its focus to cognitive accessibility, acknowledging the diversity in cognitive abilities among individuals. This involves creating environments that are easy to navigate, minimizing sensory overload, and providing clear and simple information. For instance, wayfinding systems with clear signage, simple language, and consistent visual cues benefit individuals with cognitive differences. Inclusive design strives to make spaces welcoming and user-friendly for everyone, regardless of their cognitive abilities.

Sensory Considerations: Addressing Visual and Auditory Needs

Sensory considerations are integral to inclusive design, recognizing the importance of addressing visual and auditory needs. In spaces designed with inclusivity in mind, there is a thoughtful approach to lighting, color contrast, and acoustics. Bright and evenly distributed lighting benefits individuals with visual impairments, while effective acoustics cater to those with hearing impairments. Creating environments that balance sensory inputs contributes to a more comfortable and inclusive experience for all users.

Inclusive Outdoor Spaces: Nature for Everyone

Inclusive design is not limited to indoor spaces; it extends to outdoor environments as well. In parks, recreational areas, and public spaces, inclusive design principles are applied to ensure that nature is accessible to everyone. This involves providing wheelchair-accessible pathways, inclusive playground equipment, and seating options that accommodate various needs. By making outdoor spaces inclusive, individuals of all abilities can enjoy the benefits of nature and community engagement.

Technological Integration for Accessibility

Advancements in technology play a pivotal role in inclusive design. From smart city technologies to assistive devices, technology contributes to creating more accessible and inclusive environments. For example, mobile applications that provide real-time navigation for individuals with visual impairments enhance their ability to independently navigate urban spaces. Similarly, hearing loops in public spaces support individuals with hearing impairments by delivering clear audio signals directly to their hearing aids.

Housing for All: Inclusive Residential Design

Inclusive design principles extend to residential spaces, ensuring that homes are designed to accommodate the diverse needs of individuals and families. Features such as zero-step entrances, wider doorways, and adaptable spaces benefit individuals with mobility challenges. Inclusive kitchens with adjustable countertops and accessible storage options enhance the functionality of the space for everyone. By incorporating inclusive design into residential architecture, homes become spaces where individuals of all abilities can live comfortably and independently.

Workplace Inclusivity: Enabling Professional Participation

The principles of inclusive design are crucial in workplace environments to enable professional participation for individuals of all abilities. Inclusive office spaces consider features such as adjustable desks, accessible meeting rooms, and technology accommodations to support employees with diverse needs. By fostering an inclusive workplace, organizations not only comply with legal requirements but also create environments that value diversity and maximize the potential of their workforce.

Accessible Transportation: Removing Mobility Barriers

Inclusive design in transportation focuses on removing barriers to mobility. This involves designing accessible public transit systems, providing options like low-floor buses and accessible subway stations. Inclusive transportation considers the needs of individuals with varying abilities, ensuring that everyone can independently and comfortably navigate the urban landscape. From accessible sidewalks to well-designed transit hubs, inclusive transportation promotes equality in mobility.

Community Engagement in Design

An essential aspect of inclusive design is engaging the community in the design process. By involving individuals with diverse abilities, as well as representatives from various demographic groups, designers can gain valuable insights into the specific needs of the community. This participatory approach ensures that the design reflects the lived experiences and aspirations of the people it aims to serve, contributing to the creation of truly inclusive and responsive spaces.

Inclusive Design in Cultural and Entertainment Spaces

Cultural and entertainment venues play a vital role in community life, and inclusive design principles are essential in making these spaces accessible to everyone. This involves providing inclusive seating arrangements, accessible restrooms, and sensory-friendly features. Inclusive design in cultural spaces ensures that individuals of all abilities can participate in and enjoy cultural events, fostering a sense of community and shared experiences.

Challenges and Considerations

Incorporating inclusive design principles into urban development and architecture comes with challenges. Limited awareness and understanding of inclusive design, coupled with budget constraints, can pose hurdles to implementation. Striking a balance between diverse needs and preferences within a community may require creative solutions and compromise. Additionally, evolving technologies and design standards demand ongoing education and adaptation to ensure that spaces remain inclusive and up-to-date.

Summary

Inclusive design stands as a transformative force in urban development, reshaping spaces to be welcoming, accessible, and enriching for individuals of all abilities. By going beyond physical accessibility to embrace cognitive, sensory, and cultural inclusivity, inclusive design contributes to the creation of environments where diversity is celebrated, equality is prioritized, and the well-being of communities is enhanced. As cities continue to evolve, the principles of inclusive design offer a roadmap to building a more inclusive, compassionate, and equitable urban landscape where everyone can thrive.

Cultural Influences on Holistic Architecture

Architecture is more than a manifestation of form and function; it is deeply intertwined with the cultural fabric of societies. The chapter on "Cultural Influences on Holistic Architecture" explores the profound impact of culture on the design, function, and perception of spaces. Holistic architecture, with its emphasis on well-being and harmony, is particularly responsive to cultural influences, drawing inspiration from traditions, beliefs, and societal values to create environments that resonate with the people they serve.

Roots of Cultural Influences in Architecture

Architecture, as an expression of human creativity and necessity, has always been shaped by cultural influences. The design of dwellings, communal spaces, and sacred structures has been profoundly influenced by the values, customs, and beliefs of different societies throughout history. Whether manifested in the intricate carvings of ancient temples, the minimalist aesthetics of Japanese tea houses, or the vibrant colors of Moroccan architecture, cultural influences leave an indelible mark on the built environment.

Interplay of Tradition and Modernity

Holistic architecture navigates the delicate interplay between tradition and modernity, drawing from cultural roots while responding to contemporary needs. This approach acknowledges that culture is not static but a dynamic force that evolves over time. Architects engaged in holistic design often seek to integrate traditional elements, such as materials, spatial arrangements, or symbolic motifs, into modern structures. This fusion of tradition and modernity aims to create spaces that honor cultural heritage while embracing the requirements of contemporary living.

Sacred Spaces: Expressions of Belief Systems

Cultural influences are particularly palpable in the design of sacred spaces, such as temples, churches, mosques, and shrines. These structures often serve as architectural embodiments of religious or spiritual beliefs, reflecting the cosmology, rituals, and symbolism of a particular culture. Holistic architects, when designing sacred spaces, delve into the cultural nuances of the community, incorporating elements that evoke a sense of reverence and spiritual connection. The design of sacred spaces in holistic architecture becomes a dialogue between the divine and the cultural identity of the community.

Regional Vernacular Architecture

Holistic architecture is keenly attuned to regional vernacular architecture, embracing the traditional building styles and materials of a particular area. Vernacular architecture is a reflection of the local climate, available resources, and cultural practices. Holistic architects leverage this knowledge to create buildings that seamlessly integrate with their natural and cultural surroundings. Whether it's adobe structures in arid regions, stilt houses in coastal areas, or timber cabins in forested landscapes, the regional vernacular becomes a source of inspiration for holistic design.

Cultural Symbolism in Design

Cultural influences infuse architecture with symbolism, enriching spaces with meanings that resonate with the community. Symbolic elements may include motifs, colors, or architectural features that carry cultural significance. For example, the use of auspicious symbols in East Asian architecture or the incorporation of geometric patterns in Islamic architecture. In holistic design, these symbolic elements are carefully integrated to not only convey cultural meanings but also to evoke positive emotions and a sense of connection among inhabitants.

Harmony with Nature in Indigenous Cultures

Indigenous cultures often embody a deep connection with nature, viewing the environment as a living entity with which they coexist. Holistic architecture, influenced by such cultures, places a strong emphasis on creating harmony between built spaces and the natural world. Designs may incorporate sustainable materials, natural lighting, and open layouts that blur the boundaries between indoor and outdoor spaces. In doing so, holistic architects draw inspiration from indigenous wisdom, fostering a symbiotic relationship between the built environment and the natural ecosystem.

Courtyards, Gardens, and Open Spaces

Cultural influences shape the design of open spaces within holistic architecture, with an emphasis on courtyards, gardens, and communal areas. In many cultures, these spaces serve as central gathering points for social interactions, celebrations, and communal activities. Holistic architects, informed by cultural practices, integrate these elements to create environments that foster a sense of community, well-being, and connection to nature. The arrangement of spaces reflects cultural preferences for socializing, contemplation, and recreation.

Adapting to Cultural Diversity

In an era of globalization and cultural diversity, holistic architecture embraces the challenge of creating spaces that cater to varied cultural perspectives. The design process involves a deep understanding of the cultural mosaic within a community or urban setting. Holistic architects navigate the nuances of multiculturalism, creating environments that are inclusive, respectful, and responsive to the diverse needs and values of the people they serve.

Celebrating Festivals and Rituals

Cultural influences manifest vividly during festivals and rituals, and holistic architecture often responds to these occasions. Whether designing temporary structures for festivals, spaces for communal rituals, or buildings that host cultural events, architects incorporate elements that enhance the celebratory atmosphere. The spatial design considers the flow of people, the significance of rituals, and the cultural symbolism associated with specific festivities.

Materiality and Craftsmanship

Cultural influences profoundly impact the material choices and craftsmanship embraced in holistic architecture. Traditional building materials and construction techniques carry cultural histories and embody local wisdom. Holistic architects, attuned to these influences, may prioritize the use of indigenous materials, traditional craftsmanship, and locally sourced resources. This not only contributes to the sustainability of the built environment but also preserves cultural practices and supports local economies.

Cultural Sensitivity in Globalized Settings

In an era where architectural projects often transcend cultural boundaries, cultural sensitivity becomes a critical aspect of holistic design. Architects navigate the delicate balance of creating spaces that are culturally resonant while being inclusive and respectful of diverse backgrounds. This requires a nuanced understanding of the cultural nuances within a globalized context, ensuring that the design fosters a sense of belonging for individuals from various cultural backgrounds.

Challenges and Considerations

While cultural influences enrich holistic architecture, they also present challenges. Balancing authenticity with modern functionality, addressing cultural appropriation concerns, and accommodating diverse cultural perspectives within a community can be complex. Additionally, architects must navigate cultural sensitivities and avoid imposing their own biases on the design. Successful navigation of these challenges requires open communication, community engagement, and a commitment to cultural competence.

Summary

"Cultural Influences on Holistic Architecture" underscores the profound impact of cultural contexts on the design and experience of built environments. From the symbolism embedded in sacred spaces to the adaptability of vernacular architecture, cultural influences shape the narrative of holistic architecture. By embracing cultural diversity, respecting local traditions, and weaving cultural symbolism into design, holistic architecture becomes a vibrant tapestry that reflects the values, identity, and well-being of the communities it serves. As architects continue to navigate the interplay of culture and design, holistic architecture stands as a testament to the rich interconnection between the built environment and the cultural heritage of humanity.

The Impact of Architecture on Mental Health

Architecture, beyond its aesthetic and functional dimensions, plays a profound role in shaping the mental well-being of individuals. This chapter delves into the intricate relationship between architecture and mental health, exploring how design principles, spatial arrangements, and environmental factors can significantly influence emotional states, stress levels, and overall psychological well-being.

The Built Environment as a Psychological Canvas

From the bustling urban landscapes to the serenity of natural retreats, the built environment serves as a canvas that either nurtures or challenges mental health. Architects, knowingly or unknowingly, wield the power to shape spaces that evoke emotions, trigger memories, and influence cognitive processes. Understanding the psychological impact of architecture is essential in creating environments that contribute positively to mental well-being.

Biophilic Design and Connection with Nature

Biophilic design, rooted in the innate human connection with nature, is a cornerstone of promoting mental health through architecture. Incorporating natural elements, such as plants, natural light, and water features, into the built environment has been shown to reduce stress, enhance cognitive function, and improve overall mood. Buildings that embrace biophilic principles create a harmonious interplay between the artificial and the natural, fostering a sense of tranquility and well-being.

Daylight and Circadian Rhythms

Natural light, with its dynamic qualities, has a profound impact on circadian rhythms and, consequently, mental health. Exposure to natural light influences the production of melatonin and serotonin, hormones that regulate sleep and mood. Architectural designs that maximize daylight penetration into indoor spaces contribute to better sleep patterns, improved mood, and enhanced overall mental health. Balancing the use of artificial lighting to mimic natural patterns further supports circadian alignment.

Spatial Layouts and Flow for Stress Reduction

The layout and flow of spaces within built environments can significantly affect stress levels and mental well-being. Open, flexible layouts that promote easy navigation and visual connectivity contribute to a sense of spaciousness and reduce feelings of confinement. Conversely, overcrowded or maze-like structures can induce stress and anxiety. Architects, through thoughtful spatial planning, can create environments that encourage relaxation, social interaction, and a sense of control over one's surroundings.

Privacy and Personal Space

The need for privacy and personal space is a fundamental aspect of mental well-being. Architecture that respects and integrates private spaces within communal settings supports individuals in managing stress and maintaining emotional balance. Whether it's designing quiet corners in office spaces or incorporating secluded nooks in residential settings, architects play a crucial role in crafting environments that allow for moments of introspection and solitude.

Color Psychology in Architectural Design

Colors have a profound impact on mood and emotions, a principle well-acknowledged in color psychology. Architects leverage this understanding to create environments that elicit specific emotional responses. For example, cool tones such as blues and greens are often associated with calmness and tranquility, while warmer tones like yellows and oranges evoke feelings of energy and warmth. Thoughtful selection and application of colors contribute to the creation of atmospheres that support positive mental states.

Acoustics and Soundscapes

The auditory environment is another dimension of architecture that can significantly influence mental health. Excessive noise, whether from traffic, construction, or other sources, has been linked to stress and anxiety. Architects can mitigate these negative effects through sound-absorbing materials, strategic building placement, and the incorporation of natural sounds, such as running water or birdsong. Creating spaces with balanced acoustics contributes to a more calming and conducive mental environment.

Therapeutic Design in Healthcare Settings

In healthcare architecture, the principles of therapeutic design play a crucial role in enhancing the mental well-being of patients. Elements such as access to natural light, views of nature, and the use of soothing colors contribute to the healing environment. Patient rooms designed with privacy, comfort, and a connection to the outdoors have been shown to positively impact recovery rates and reduce stress. Therapeutic design extends beyond hospitals to other healthcare settings, acknowledging the psychological impact of the built environment on well-being.

Inclusive and Accessible Design

The mental well-being of individuals is intricately tied to their sense of inclusion and accessibility within the built environment. Inclusive design principles ensure that spaces are accessible to people of all abilities, fostering a sense of belonging and reducing potential stressors related to physical limitations. Thoughtful design considerations, such as ramps, elevators, and sensory-friendly features, contribute to environments that support diverse needs and promote mental well-being.

Holistic Wellness Spaces

The emergence of wellness architecture reflects a growing recognition of the interconnectedness between physical and mental health. Wellness spaces prioritize the integration of elements that address both physical and psychological well-being. From meditation rooms and fitness facilities to spaces designed for relaxation and reflection, architects are increasingly creating environments that holistically support the overall wellness of individuals.

Adaptive Reuse and Mental Well-being

The practice of adaptive reuse, transforming existing structures for new purposes, can positively impact mental well-being. Preserving historical buildings and repurposing them for contemporary use not only contributes to a sense of cultural continuity but also creates unique and character-filled spaces. Adaptive reuse projects often incorporate elements of nostalgia and authenticity, which can evoke positive emotions and contribute to a sense of well-being.

Community Spaces and Social Interaction

Architecture plays a vital role in shaping community spaces that foster social interaction and a sense of belonging. From public parks and plazas to community centers and shared workspaces, the design of spaces influences the opportunities for social engagement. Buildings that facilitate social interaction contribute to the formation of supportive communities, which, in turn, positively impact mental health by reducing feelings of isolation and loneliness.

Urban Planning and Mental Health

At the urban planning level, architecture influences the mental health of entire communities. Access to green spaces, walkable neighborhoods, and the availability of cultural and recreational amenities all play roles in community well-being. Urban planning that prioritizes mental health considerations contributes to the creation of cities and neighborhoods that support the holistic well-being of their residents.

Challenges and Considerations

While architecture holds immense potential to positively impact mental health, challenges exist. These include budget constraints, zoning regulations, and the need for interdisciplinary collaboration between architects, psychologists, and urban planners. Additionally, the subjective nature of individual experiences poses a challenge in designing universally supportive environments. Navigating these complexities requires a holistic approach that considers diverse perspectives and collaborates across disciplines.

Summary

"The Impact of Architecture on Mental Health" underscores the profound influence that built environments exert on the psychological well-being of individuals and communities. From the incorporation of biophilic design principles to the creation of therapeutic healthcare spaces, architects have the power to shape environments that either contribute to stress and anxiety or foster relaxation and connection. As the understanding of this intricate relationship continues to evolve, architects play a pivotal role in crafting spaces that prioritize mental health, contributing to a more compassionate, supportive, and well-balanced built environment.

Sustainable Landscaping for Holistic Living

In the pursuit of holistic living, the integration of sustainable landscaping emerges as a vital component that harmonizes with the natural environment, promotes ecological balance, and enhances the overall well-being of individuals and communities. This chapter explores the principles and practices of sustainable landscaping, illustrating how thoughtful design and eco-friendly approaches contribute to a holistic way of living.

Foundations of Sustainable Landscaping

Sustainable landscaping is rooted in principles that prioritize the health of ecosystems, minimize environmental impact, and contribute to the overall well-being of inhabitants. At its core, it goes beyond conventional landscaping practices, recognizing the interconnectedness of natural systems and the importance of coexistence with the environment.

1. Biodiversity Conservation: Sustainable landscaping seeks to preserve and enhance biodiversity by selecting native plants, creating habitats for wildlife, and promoting a balanced ecosystem. Native plants are adapted to local conditions, requiring less water and maintenance, while also providing food and shelter for local fauna. This approach fosters a healthier and more resilient environment.

2. Water Conservation: Water scarcity is a global concern, and sustainable landscaping addresses this challenge by prioritizing water-efficient practices. This includes the use of drought-resistant plants, rainwater harvesting systems, and permeable surfaces that allow water to infiltrate the soil. By minimizing water consumption, sustainable landscaping contributes to the conservation of this precious resource.

3. Soil Health and Restoration: Healthy soil is fundamental to sustainable landscaping. Techniques such as composting, mulching, and using organic fertilizers enhance soil fertility and structure. Additionally, sustainable landscaping avoids the use of harmful pesticides and chemicals, promoting a natural balance of beneficial organisms in the soil. Soil health not only supports plant growth but also plays a crucial role in overall ecosystem vitality.

4. Energy Efficiency: Landscaping decisions can impact the energy efficiency of buildings. Thoughtful placement of trees and shrubs can provide shade, reducing the need for air conditioning in warmer months. Windbreaks and strategic planting can also mitigate heat loss in colder climates. By considering the energy dynamics of the landscape, sustainable design contributes to the overall efficiency of the built environment.

5. Permaculture Principles: Permaculture, a design approach that mimics natural ecosystems, is often integrated into sustainable landscaping. This includes the creation of food forests, companion planting, and the utilization of natural patterns to optimize resource use. Permaculture principles not only contribute to sustainable food production but also enhance the resilience and diversity of landscapes.

Designing Holistic Outdoor Spaces

Sustainable landscaping goes hand in hand with the creation of outdoor spaces that support holistic living. These spaces are not merely ornamental but serve as extensions of living environments, providing opportunities for relaxation, recreation, and connection with nature. The design of such spaces incorporates elements that cater to physical, mental, and emotional well-being.

1. Outdoor Retreats: Sustainable landscaping often includes the creation of outdoor retreats that serve as havens for relaxation and contemplation. These spaces may feature comfortable seating, native plantings, and elements that engage the senses, such as water features or aromatic plants. Outdoor retreats provide a respite from the demands of daily life, promoting mental and emotional well-being.

2. Edible Landscaping: Integrating edible plants into landscaping design aligns with the principles of sustainability and contributes to a holistic lifestyle. Fruit trees, vegetable gardens, and herb beds become functional elements of the landscape, providing fresh, nutritious produce. This not only promotes self-sufficiency but also connects inhabitants with the cycles of nature and the joy of growing their own food.

3. Mindful Pathways: Sustainable landscaping embraces the concept of mindful pathways, designed to encourage contemplative walks and a sense of connection with the environment. Pathways may wind through gardens, meadows, or wooded areas, providing opportunities for individuals to engage with nature and experience the therapeutic benefits of outdoor spaces. Mindful pathways contribute to the overall well-being by fostering a sense of tranquility and mindfulness.

4. Gathering Spaces: Communal gathering spaces are integral to holistic living, and sustainable landscaping designs them to be environmentally conscious and socially engaging. Whether it's a community garden, a shared outdoor kitchen, or a shaded seating area, these spaces encourage social interactions, community bonding, and a shared appreciation for the natural surroundings. Sustainable materials and energy-efficient lighting further enhance the eco-friendly aspect of these spaces.

5. Play and Recreation Areas: Sustainable landscaping recognizes the importance of play and recreation in holistic living, especially for families and communities. Play areas may incorporate natural elements like boulders and logs, and recreational spaces might include eco-friendly features such as permeable play surfaces. Prioritizing the well-being of children and adults alike, these areas contribute to physical fitness, social connection, and overall community vitality.

Green Infrastructure and Urban Resilience

In urban settings, sustainable landscaping extends beyond individual properties to encompass green infrastructure that enhances the resilience of entire communities. The integration of green spaces, permeable surfaces, and sustainable stormwater management systems contributes to urban ecosystems that are not only environmentally responsible but also conducive to holistic living.

1. Urban Parks and Green Belts: The inclusion of urban parks and green belts within city planning reflects a commitment to sustainable landscaping. These areas serve as lungs for urban environments, providing oxygen, absorbing pollutants, and offering recreational spaces for residents. The presence of greenery in urban settings contributes to improved air quality and mental well-being.

2. Sustainable Stormwater Management: Traditional stormwater management systems can contribute to pollution and environmental degradation. Sustainable landscaping, however, embraces techniques such as rain gardens, permeable pavements, and green roofs to manage stormwater in an eco-friendly manner. These practices mitigate flooding, protect water quality, and enhance the overall resilience of urban areas.

3. Green Roofs and Walls: The incorporation of green roofs and walls into architectural design is a manifestation of sustainable landscaping in urban environments. These features not only provide insulation, reducing energy consumption, but also contribute to biodiversity and aesthetic enhancement. Green roofs and walls are emblematic of the integration of nature into the urban fabric, promoting a more sustainable and holistic way of living.

4. Community Gardens and Urban Farming: Sustainable landscaping in urban areas often includes the creation of community gardens and urban farming initiatives. These spaces empower residents to actively engage with the cultivation of their food, fostering a sense of community, promoting sustainability, and connecting urban dwellers with the natural cycles of growth and harvest.

5. Eco-friendly Streetscapes: Streetscapes designed with sustainability in mind contribute to the overall environmental quality of urban areas. Sustainable landscaping principles are applied to street tree plantings, green medians, and pedestrian-friendly zones. These features enhance the aesthetics of urban spaces, reduce heat island effects, and create more pleasant environments for residents.

Challenges and Considerations

While the principles of sustainable landscaping align with holistic living, there are challenges in their implementation. These challenges include balancing aesthetic preferences with ecological considerations, navigating regulatory constraints, and overcoming initial costs associated with sustainable practices. Additionally, educating communities about the benefits of sustainable landscaping is crucial to fostering widespread adoption.

Summary

"Sustainable Landscaping for Holistic Living" underscores the transformative potential of integrating sustainable landscaping practices into the fabric of our living environments. From preserving biodiversity and conserving water to creating mindful outdoor spaces and promoting urban resilience, sustainable landscaping contributes to a holistic way of living that prioritizes the well-being of individuals and communities. As we continue to navigate the complexities of modern living, the principles of sustainable landscaping stand as a beacon, guiding us toward a more harmonious and interconnected relationship with the natural world.

Water Features and Their Calming Effects

Water, with its mesmerizing qualities and inherent connection to the natural world, has long been recognized for its ability to evoke a sense of calm and tranquility. This chapter explores the profound impact of water features on mental well-being, delving into the various types of water features, their design principles, and the therapeutic effects they bring to the built environment.

The Timeless Allure of Water

From ancient civilizations to modern landscapes, the allure of water has transcended time and cultural boundaries. The presence of water has been associated with life, renewal, and a sense of peace. Water features, ranging from intricate fountains to serene ponds, tap into this universal appreciation for water, creating environments that resonate with our innate connection to the natural world.

1. Fountains: Fountains are perhaps the most iconic and versatile water features, gracing public squares, gardens, and interior spaces. The gentle flow of water, whether in cascading tiers or dancing sprays, has an immediate calming effect. The rhythmic sound of water falling creates a soothing auditory experience, while the visual spectacle of dancing water droplets engages the senses, fostering a sense of serenity.

2. Ponds and Lakes: Natural water bodies, such as ponds and lakes, contribute to a holistic and serene environment. The stillness of a pond or the gentle ripples on a lake's surface induces a meditative atmosphere. The reflection of surrounding elements on the water's surface adds an aesthetic dimension, creating a harmonious blend of nature and built structures.

3. Waterfalls: The dynamic energy of waterfalls, whether in natural landscapes or designed features, adds a touch of drama to the environment. The sound of cascading water, combined with the visual spectacle of a waterfall, creates a multisensory experience. Waterfalls are often incorporated into landscaping to introduce a sense of movement and to amplify the calming effects associated with flowing water.

4. Reflecting Pools: Reflecting pools, characterized by calm, mirror-like surfaces, add an element of contemplation to spaces. Often placed in proximity to architectural structures, these pools reflect the surrounding environment, creating a visual connection between the built and natural elements. The stillness of reflecting pools fosters a tranquil ambiance conducive to reflection and relaxation.

5. Streams and Water Channels: Incorporating meandering streams or water channels into landscapes mimics the gentle flow of natural watercourses. The sound of water trickling over stones and the visual continuity of a flowing stream contribute to a sense of continuity and connection with nature. These features are often integrated into garden designs to enhance the overall calming atmosphere.

Design Principles for Calming Water Features

The design of water features plays a pivotal role in maximizing their calming effects. Thoughtful consideration of aesthetics, scale, and integration with the surrounding environment enhances the overall impact of water features on mental well-being.

1. Aesthetic Harmony: The aesthetic harmony between water features and their surroundings is essential for creating a calming atmosphere. Whether situated in a contemporary urban plaza or a traditional garden, the design of water features should complement the architectural style and natural elements of the environment. Harmonious design fosters a seamless integration that feels both purposeful and serene.

2. Scale and Proportion: The scale and proportion of water features are critical considerations. Features that are too large for a space may feel overwhelming, while those that are too small might lack the desired impact. Achieving the right balance ensures that water features enhance the environment without dominating it, contributing to a sense of proportionate tranquility.

3. Soundscapes: The auditory experience of water features significantly contributes to their calming effects. The sound of water, whether a gentle trickle or a cascading flow, creates a natural and soothing soundtrack. The design should consider the acoustics of the space, ensuring that the water's sound complements the environment and contributes to a harmonious soundscape.

4. Integration with Nature: Water features, when integrated with natural elements, enhance the overall sense of calm. Incorporating lush vegetation, natural stones, and appropriate landscaping around water features creates a holistic environment. This integration with nature promotes a sense of authenticity and organic beauty, elevating the calming impact of the water feature.

5. Lighting Effects: Strategic lighting can enhance the visual appeal of water features, extending their calming effects into the evening. Illuminating water features creates a play of light and shadow, adding a magical quality to the environment. The gentle reflection of light on the water's surface further contributes to the calming ambiance, creating a tranquil and enchanting atmosphere.

6. Accessibility and Interaction: The accessibility and interactive potential of water features are essential considerations, especially in public spaces. Features that invite interaction, such as stepping stones or shallow pools, engage visitors in a multisensory experience. The ability to physically connect with the water feature fosters a sense of connection and involvement, contributing to the overall calming atmosphere.

Therapeutic Effects of Water Features

The calming effects of water features extend beyond aesthetics, influencing mental and emotional well-being. Research has explored the therapeutic benefits associated with exposure to water features, shedding light on the mechanisms through which these features positively impact individuals.

1. Stress Reduction: One of the most well-documented benefits of water features is their ability to reduce stress. The sound of flowing water has been shown to lower cortisol levels, a key indicator of stress, leading to a calmer physiological state. Whether in the form of a fountain, waterfall, or gentle stream, the presence of water contributes to stress reduction and relaxation.

2. Improved Mood: Exposure to water features has been linked to improvements in mood and emotional well-being. The visual and auditory stimuli provided by water features trigger the release of neurotransmitters associated with pleasure and mood enhancement. Individuals often report feeling more positive, relaxed, and content in environments featuring well-designed water features.

3. Enhanced Cognitive Function: The calming effects of water extend to cognitive function. Studies suggest that exposure to natural elements, including water, can improve cognitive performance and attention restoration. Individuals in environments with water features have demonstrated increased focus, better problem-solving abilities, and a greater capacity for mental clarity.

4. Sleep Quality: The calming influence of water features can positively impact sleep quality. The soothing sounds of water can create a conducive environment for relaxation, helping individuals unwind and prepare for restful sleep. Water features, whether indoors or outdoors, contribute to a calming bedtime routine that supports overall sleep hygiene.

5. Mindfulness and Meditation: Water features provide an ideal backdrop for mindfulness and meditation practices. The gentle movement and sound of water create a conducive environment for individuals seeking moments of introspection and contemplation. Water features in garden settings, for example, become focal points for mindfulness practices, promoting a sense of inner peace.

Incorporating Water Features in Various Settings

The versatility of water features allows them to be integrated into a wide range of settings, from residential gardens to public spaces and commercial environments. Each setting presents an opportunity to leverage the calming effects of water features in unique and purposeful ways.

1. Residential Gardens: In residential settings, water features become focal points that enhance the overall ambiance of outdoor spaces. Whether it's a small pond, a cascading waterfall, or a tranquil fountain, these features create intimate retreats for relaxation and reflection. The incorporation of water features into residential gardens transforms outdoor spaces into sanctuaries of calm.

2. Public Plazas and Urban Spaces: Water features in public plazas and urban spaces contribute to the vibrancy and livability of city environments. Fountains and reflecting pools become gathering points, providing respite from the urban hustle. The calming effects of water features in these settings create opportunities for social interaction, relaxation, and a sense of connection with the community.

3. Healthcare and Healing Environments: In healthcare settings, water features play a therapeutic role in supporting the healing process. Healing gardens with reflective pools or indoor fountains in medical facilities create environments that contribute to patient well-being. The calming effects of water features become integral components of holistic healthcare design, promoting comfort and reducing anxiety.

4. Corporate Environments: In corporate environments, water features contribute to the creation of more inviting and stress-reducing spaces. Indoor fountains or exterior water features in office complexes provide employees with moments of respite, fostering a positive work environment. The calming effects of water contribute to increased employee well-being and productivity.

5. Educational Institutions: Water features in educational settings, such as university campuses or school courtyards, create environments conducive to learning and relaxation. Integrating water features into educational landscapes contributes to a positive atmosphere, providing students and faculty with spaces for contemplation and rejuvenation.

Challenges and Considerations

While water features offer numerous benefits for mental well-being, their design and implementation require careful consideration of various factors.

1. Maintenance and Sustainability: Water features necessitate ongoing maintenance to ensure their optimal functioning and aesthetic appeal. Sustainable practices, such as water recycling systems and energy-efficient pumps, are essential to minimize environmental impact. Balancing the desire for elaborate features with the practicalities of maintenance is a key consideration.

2. Safety Considerations: In public spaces and residential settings, safety is paramount. Incorporating safety measures, such as non-slip surfaces, secure barriers, and shallow areas, is crucial to prevent accidents, especially in settings with children or vulnerable populations.

3. Local Regulations: Local regulations and permits may dictate the design and installation of water features. Compliance with these regulations ensures that water features align with environmental and safety standards. Engaging with local authorities and obtaining necessary approvals is a critical step in the implementation process.

4. Climate Considerations: Climate plays a significant role in the design and maintenance of water features. Harsh weather conditions, freezing temperatures, or extreme heat can impact the functionality and longevity of water features. Designing features that are resilient to local climate conditions ensures their year-round appeal.

Summary

"Water Features and Their Calming Effects" explores the timeless connection between water and human well-being, examining the design principles and therapeutic benefits associated with water features. From the rhythmic flow of fountains to the reflective tranquility of ponds, water features contribute to the creation of environments that foster relaxation, reduce stress, and enhance overall mental and emotional well-being. As architects, designers, and urban planners continue to integrate water features into diverse settings, they play a pivotal role in shaping environments that resonate with the soothing essence of water, promoting a holistic and tranquil way of living.

Holistic Approaches to Workplace Design

The workplace, once perceived solely as a functional environment for conducting business, is undergoing a transformative evolution. Holistic approaches to workplace design recognize that the physical environment profoundly impacts employee well-being, productivity, and overall satisfaction. This chapter explores the principles and strategies of holistic workplace design, delving into aspects such as spatial layout, wellness initiatives, and the integration of nature, all aimed at creating work environments that prioritize the holistic needs of employees.

Understanding Holistic Workplace Design

Holistic workplace design is founded on the principle that the workplace is not just a backdrop for business activities but a dynamic and influential factor in the lives of those who inhabit it. Recognizing the interconnectedness of physical, mental, and social well-being, holistic approaches aim to create environments that support the holistic needs of employees, fostering a sense of purpose, engagement, and overall satisfaction.

1. Spatial Layout for Collaboration and Focus: One of the key considerations in holistic workplace design is the spatial layout that balances collaboration and focused work. Open office designs promote collaboration and spontaneous interactions, fostering a sense of community. However, it's crucial to incorporate quiet zones or private spaces where employees can retreat for focused tasks, ensuring a harmonious balance between collaboration and individual productivity.

2. Biophilic Design for Well-being: Biophilic design, which integrates natural elements into the built environment, is a cornerstone of holistic workplace design. Incorporating indoor plants, natural light, and views of nature has been shown to reduce stress, enhance creativity, and improve overall well-being. Biophilic design connects employees with the natural world, creating a more harmonious and supportive work environment.

3. Ergonomics and Comfort: The physical well-being of employees is paramount in holistic workplace design. Ergonomic furniture, adjustable workstations, and comfortable seating contribute to a healthy and supportive work environment. Attention to ergonomics not only enhances physical comfort but also prevents long-term health issues, promoting overall well-being.

4. Flexible Workspaces: Holistic workplace design acknowledges the diverse needs and workstyles of employees. Flexible workspaces, including hot-desking options, collaborative zones, and quiet rooms, provide employees with the autonomy to choose environments that suit their tasks and preferences. This flexibility enhances employee satisfaction and accommodates the evolving nature of work.

5. Wellness Programs and Fitness Facilities: Incorporating wellness programs and on-site fitness facilities into workplace design reflects a commitment to the holistic health of employees. Fitness centers, yoga studios, and wellness initiatives contribute to physical health, reduce stress, and create a positive workplace culture that values the overall well-being of individuals.

6. Mindful Break Areas: Designing mindful break areas encourages employees to take breaks that contribute to their mental well-being. Comfortable seating, natural light, and elements like indoor water features or greenery create spaces where employees can recharge, fostering a sense of relaxation and mental rejuvenation.

7. Inclusive and Diverse Spaces: Holistic workplace design embraces inclusivity and diversity by creating spaces that cater to the needs of a diverse workforce. Inclusive design considerations include accessible facilities, gender-neutral spaces, and cultural elements that celebrate diversity. This approach ensures that the workplace is welcoming and supportive for all employees.

8. Technology Integration: Holistic workplace design considers the seamless integration of technology to enhance productivity and well-being. This includes providing ergonomic and technologically advanced workstations, as well as creating spaces equipped for virtual collaboration and remote work. Thoughtful technology integration supports the modern work landscape and contributes to a positive work experience.

9. Personalization and Identity: Empowering employees to personalize their workspace fosters a sense of ownership and identity. Holistic workplace design allows for customization, enabling individuals to add personal touches to their workstations. This approach creates a more personalized and empowering work environment, contributing to a sense of belonging and well-being.

10. Noise Management and Acoustics: Considering the acoustics of the workplace is crucial for employee well-being. Holistic design incorporates sound-absorbing materials, strategic placement of dividers, and designated quiet areas to manage noise levels. Creating environments that balance collaboration and concentration helps mitigate stress and supports overall mental well-being.

Implementing Holistic Workplace Design

1. Employee Involvement: A key aspect of implementing holistic workplace design is involving employees in the process. Surveys, workshops, and feedback sessions help identify the unique needs and preferences of the workforce. Engaging employees in the design process fosters a sense of ownership and ensures that the workplace aligns with their holistic well-being.

2. Collaboration with Wellness Experts: Collaborating with wellness experts, including psychologists, nutritionists, and fitness professionals, enhances the holistic approach to workplace design. Integrating expert insights into wellness programs, ergonomic considerations, and mental health initiatives ensures a comprehensive and evidence-based approach to employee well-being.

3. Continuous Evaluation and Adaptation: Holistic workplace design is an ongoing process that requires continuous evaluation and adaptation. Regular assessments of employee satisfaction, well-being, and productivity provide valuable insights. This iterative approach allows organizations to refine the workplace environment based on evolving needs and emerging trends.

4. Leadership Commitment: Leadership commitment is integral to the success of holistic workplace design. When organizational leaders prioritize employee well-being and actively support the implementation of holistic design principles, it sets a positive tone for the entire workplace culture. Leadership commitment is crucial for fostering a holistic approach that permeates throughout the organization.

5. Integration of Technology Solutions: Leveraging technology solutions that support holistic workplace design enhances the overall employee experience. This includes implementing smart building technologies for climate control, lighting, and space utilization. Integrating wellness apps and digital platforms for mental health resources further supports the holistic well-being of employees.

Measuring the Impact of Holistic Workplace Design

Quantifying the impact of holistic workplace design requires a multidimensional approach that considers various metrics related to employee well-being, engagement, and organizational performance.

1. Employee Satisfaction Surveys: Regular employee satisfaction surveys are valuable tools for gauging the impact of holistic workplace design. These surveys can include questions about workspace comfort, wellness initiatives, work-life balance, and overall job satisfaction. Analyzing survey results provides insights into the effectiveness of the design in meeting employee needs.

2. Productivity Metrics: Monitoring productivity metrics, such as project completion rates, time management, and collaboration effectiveness, helps assess the impact of the workplace design on work outcomes. Positive changes in productivity metrics indicate that the design is supporting employees in achieving their tasks efficiently.

3. Employee Health and Wellness Indicators: Tracking health and wellness indicators, such as absenteeism rates, stress-related incidents, and participation in wellness programs, provides a holistic view of employee well-being. Reductions in absenteeism and stress-related issues indicate that the workplace design is positively influencing health outcomes.

4. Talent Retention and Recruitment: The ability to attract and retain talent is a key indicator of the success of holistic workplace design. High employee retention rates, coupled with positive feedback from recruits about the workplace environment, reflect the desirability of the organization's approach to holistic well-being.

5. Organizational Culture and Collaboration: Observing changes in organizational culture and collaboration dynamics provides qualitative insights into the impact of holistic workplace design. Positive shifts in the workplace culture, increased collaboration, and a sense of community among employees signify that the design is fostering a supportive and cohesive work environment.

Challenges and Considerations

Implementing holistic workplace design comes with its share of challenges and considerations that organizations must navigate to ensure a successful transformation.

1. Budget Constraints: Holistic workplace design may involve initial investments in ergonomic furniture, wellness programs, and technology integration. Balancing these enhancements with budget constraints requires strategic planning and prioritization to achieve the most impactful changes within the available resources.

2. Change Management: Introducing significant changes to the workplace design necessitates effective change management. Communicating the rationale behind the changes, involving employees in the process, and addressing concerns help ease the transition. Proactive change management strategies contribute to a smoother adoption of holistic design principles.

3. Diverse Workforce Needs: A diverse workforce may have varied needs and preferences when it comes to the workplace environment. Holistic design should consider inclusivity and flexibility to accommodate the diverse requirements of employees, ensuring that the workplace is supportive for individuals with different workstyles, abilities, and preferences.

4. Technological Adaptation: Integrating technology solutions requires careful consideration of the organization's technological infrastructure and employees' comfort with digital tools. Providing adequate training and support for technology adoption ensures that the benefits of digital solutions are maximized without causing disruptions.

5. Regulatory Compliance: Adhering to regulatory standards and building codes is crucial in workplace design. Holistic design initiatives should align with legal requirements related to accessibility, safety, and environmental sustainability. Compliance with regulations ensures that the workplace is not only holistic but also meets established standards for health and safety.

Summary

"Holistic Approaches to Workplace Design" explores the transformative shift from traditional office layouts to holistic design principles that prioritize the well-being of employees. By considering spatial layouts, biophilic design, ergonomics, and wellness initiatives, organizations create work environments that foster a sense of purpose, engagement, and overall satisfaction. The implementation of holistic workplace design involves collaboration with employees, wellness experts, and a commitment to continuous evaluation and adaptation. Measuring the impact through employee surveys, productivity metrics, and organizational culture indicators provides valuable insights into the success of holistic workplace design. Despite challenges, the pursuit of holistic approaches to workplace design reflects a commitment to creating environments that go beyond functionality, contributing to the holistic well-being of individuals and the success of organizations in the evolving landscape of work.

Designing for Holistic Learning Environments

The design of educational spaces plays a pivotal role in shaping the learning experience and nurturing the holistic development of students. In this chapter, we explore the principles and strategies involved in designing holistic learning environments. From flexible layouts to the integration of technology and nature, each element contributes to an environment that fosters not only academic growth but also the overall well-being of students.

The Evolution of Learning Spaces

Traditional classrooms, characterized by rows of desks and a teacher-centered approach, are evolving into dynamic learning environments that recognize the diverse needs and learning styles of students. Holistic learning environments aim to create spaces that inspire curiosity, creativity, and a sense of community, promoting not only academic success but also the social, emotional, and physical well-being of students.

1. Flexible and Adaptable Spaces: Holistic learning environments embrace flexibility in spatial design. Fixed rows of desks are replaced with movable furniture that allows for easy reconfiguration. This adaptability accommodates various teaching methods, collaborative activities, and individual study. The ability to modify the space based on the learning needs of the moment enhances engagement and fosters a dynamic learning experience.

2. Integration of Technology: In the digital age, technology is an integral part of the learning process. Holistic learning environments seamlessly integrate technology, providing students with access to interactive displays, online resources, and collaborative tools. Smart classrooms equipped with audio-visual systems, digital whiteboards, and connectivity options enhance the educational experience and prepare students for the technology-driven world.

3. Biophilic Design Elements: Connecting students with nature is a fundamental principle of holistic learning environments. Biophilic design, which incorporates natural elements into the built environment, is employed to create a harmonious atmosphere. Large windows that bring in natural light, indoor plants, and outdoor learning spaces contribute to a positive and calming environment that supports overall well-being.

4. Collaborative Learning Hubs: Holistic learning environments prioritize collaboration as a key component of the educational experience. Designing collaborative learning hubs encourages group activities, discussions, and projects. These hubs may feature comfortable seating, writable surfaces for brainstorming, and technology interfaces for collaborative work. Creating spaces that foster collaboration nurtures teamwork, communication skills, and a sense of community.

5. Varied Learning Zones: Recognizing the diversity of learning styles, holistic environments incorporate varied learning zones. Quiet zones provide spaces for focused individual study, while interactive zones cater to collaborative activities. The inclusion of relaxation corners or breakout areas allows students to recharge mentally and emotionally. Designing spaces that cater to different learning preferences enhances the inclusivity of the learning environment.

6. Mindful Use of Color and Lighting: The use of color and lighting is thoughtfully considered in holistic learning environments. Natural and warm tones create a welcoming atmosphere, while pops of color can stimulate creativity. Adequate lighting, both natural and artificial, is crucial for maintaining focus and reducing eye strain. Mindful choices in color and lighting contribute to a visually appealing and conducive learning environment.

7. Inclusive Design for Accessibility: Holistic learning environments prioritize inclusive design to ensure accessibility for all students. This includes ramps, elevators, and accessible furniture for students with mobility challenges. Additionally, technology is leveraged to support students with diverse learning needs, ensuring that the educational environment is inclusive and supportive of every student's journey.

8. Integration of Arts and Creativity Spaces: Recognizing the importance of arts in education, holistic learning environments incorporate dedicated spaces for creativity. Art studios, music rooms, and maker spaces provide students with outlets for self-expression and hands-on learning. Integrating the arts into the learning environment fosters creativity, critical thinking, and a well-rounded educational experience.

9. Comfortable and Ergonomic Furniture: Comfortable and ergonomic furniture is a cornerstone of holistic learning environments. Students spend significant hours sitting during the school day, and the design of chairs and desks impacts their physical well-being. Ergonomic furniture supports proper posture and comfort, contributing to a positive and health-conscious learning experience.

10. Outdoor Learning Spaces: Taking learning beyond the confines of indoor classrooms, holistic environments include outdoor learning spaces. Whether it's a courtyard, garden, or dedicated outdoor classroom, these spaces provide opportunities for experiential learning, connecting with nature, and physical activity. Outdoor learning spaces contribute to a holistic approach by integrating the benefits of the natural environment into the educational experience.

Implementing Holistic Learning Environments

1. Collaborative Planning with Educators: The successful implementation of holistic learning environments involves collaboration between architects, designers, and educators. Engaging teachers in the planning process ensures that the design aligns with pedagogical goals and supports effective teaching methods. Educators' insights into the needs of students and the dynamics of the learning process are invaluable in creating environments that enhance educational outcomes.

2. Student Input and Involvement: Incorporating student input into the design process empowers them and ensures that their needs and preferences are considered. Student involvement can range from participating in design workshops to providing feedback on proposed plans. This collaborative approach fosters a sense of ownership and creates learning environments that resonate with the students.

3. Professional Development for Educators: Introducing new learning environments may require educators to adapt their teaching methods. Providing professional development opportunities for teachers ensures that they are equipped to leverage the features of the new spaces effectively. Training in technology integration, collaborative teaching strategies, and the utilization of flexible learning environments supports educators in delivering an enhanced learning experience.

4. Pilot Programs and Iterative Design: Implementing holistic learning environments can benefit from a phased approach. Piloting new designs in specific areas allows for observation, feedback, and adjustments before full-scale implementation. An iterative design process, incorporating lessons learned from pilot programs, ensures that the final learning environments are optimized for both functionality and well-being.

5. Community Engagement: Engaging the broader community in the design and implementation of holistic learning environments fosters a sense of shared responsibility and pride. This engagement may involve community workshops, open houses, and collaboration with local organizations. Including the community in the process contributes to a supportive and collaborative educational ecosystem.

Measuring the Impact of Holistic Learning Environments

Assessing the impact of holistic learning environments involves evaluating various indicators related to academic performance, student well-being, and overall satisfaction.

1. Academic Achievement: Monitoring academic performance, including grades, standardized test scores, and student progression, provides insights into the impact of holistic learning environments on educational outcomes. Positive trends in academic achievement suggest that the design is supporting effective teaching and learning practices.

2. Student Engagement and Attendance: Increased student engagement and improved attendance are indicators of a positive learning environment. Holistic learning environments that foster a sense of community, collaboration, and excitement for learning contribute to higher levels of student engagement and attendance.

3. Social and Emotional Well-being: Assessing the social and emotional well-being of students includes factors such as self-esteem, relationships, and emotional resilience. Holistic learning environments that support positive social interactions and emotional development contribute to the overall well-being of students.

4. Feedback and Surveys: Collecting feedback from students, educators, and parents through surveys provides valuable insights into their experiences with the learning environment. Questions related to comfort, engagement, and satisfaction help identify areas of success and areas for improvement in the design.

5. Graduation and Post-Graduation Outcomes: Tracking graduation rates and post-graduation outcomes, such as college enrollment and career readiness, provides a long-term perspective on the impact of holistic learning environments. Positive trends in these outcomes indicate that the educational environment has prepared students for future success.

Challenges and Considerations

Implementing holistic learning environments faces challenges that require thoughtful consideration and strategic solutions.

1. Budget Constraints: Budget limitations can pose challenges in implementing holistic learning environments. Prioritizing key elements and seeking creative solutions, such as partnerships with local organizations or utilizing existing spaces, can help maximize the impact within budget constraints.

2. Maintenance and Sustainability: Maintaining holistic learning environments requires ongoing attention to cleanliness, safety, and the longevity of design elements. Implementing sustainable practices, both in terms of materials used and energy efficiency, contributes to the long-term viability of the learning environment.

3. Cultural Sensitivity: Designing for holistic learning environments requires cultural sensitivity to ensure that the spaces are inclusive and reflective of the diverse backgrounds of students. Incorporating cultural elements and engaging with the community helps create environments that are respectful and welcoming.

4. Regulatory Compliance: Adherence to educational regulations and safety standards is critical in the design and implementation of learning environments. Holistic designs must align with building codes, accessibility requirements, and educational guidelines to ensure the well-being and safety of students and educators.

5. Continuous Evaluation and Adaptation: Holistic learning environments should be subject to continuous evaluation and adaptation. Flexibility in design allows for adjustments based on evolving educational needs, technological advancements, and feedback from the educational community. Regular assessments contribute to the ongoing optimization of learning spaces.

Summary

"Designing for Holistic Learning Environments" explores the transformative shift from traditional classrooms to dynamic, student-centered spaces that prioritize the holistic development of learners. Flexible layouts, technology integration, biophilic design, and inclusive elements contribute to environments that foster academic growth, social engagement, and overall well-being. Implementing holistic learning environments involves collaboration with educators, student input, professional development, and community engagement. Measuring the impact includes assessing academic achievement, student engagement, social and emotional well-being, and graduation outcomes. Despite challenges such as budget constraints and regulatory compliance, the pursuit of holistic learning environments reflects a commitment to creating educational spaces that nurture the potential of every student, fostering a love for learning and a holistic approach to education.

Spiritual Spaces: Architecture for the Soul

The design of spiritual spaces has transcended mere structural elements to become a profound exploration of the connection between architecture and the human soul. This chapter delves into the intricate artistry and thoughtful considerations involved in creating spaces that evoke a sense of the sacred, nurturing the spiritual well-being of those who inhabit them.

The Essence of Spiritual Spaces

Spiritual spaces, whether temples, churches, mosques, synagogues, or meditation centers, are characterized by their ability to transcend the physical realm and tap into the ethereal aspects of human existence. These spaces are designed to facilitate a deep connection with the divine, offering a sanctuary for contemplation, worship, and inner reflection. The architecture of spiritual spaces becomes a vessel for the sacred, guiding individuals on a journey of the soul.

1. Symbolism and Sacred Geometry: At the heart of spiritual architecture lies a rich tapestry of symbolism and sacred geometry. Design elements are meticulously chosen to convey profound meanings, often rooted in religious or cultural traditions. From the layout of the space to the choice of materials and the arrangement of symbols, every detail is a deliberate expression of the spiritual narrative.

2. Light as a Metaphor: Light holds profound significance in spiritual spaces, symbolizing divine presence, enlightenment, and the journey from darkness to illumination. Architects harness natural light through strategically placed windows, skylights, and openings. The interplay of light and shadow becomes a dynamic representation of the spiritual journey, creating an atmosphere that resonates with the sacred.

3. Proportion and Scale: Proportion and scale are critical considerations in the design of spiritual spaces. These elements evoke a sense of awe and reverence, emphasizing the transcendence of the divine. The height of a cathedral's nave, the intricacies of a minaret, or the harmonious proportions of a meditation hall contribute to an environment that transcends the everyday and elevates the human spirit.

4. Ritualistic Elements: Spiritual spaces often incorporate ritualistic elements that guide worshippers through a ceremonial journey. Altars, prayer niches, and ritual platforms are carefully positioned to facilitate religious practices. The arrangement of these elements is not merely functional but is choreographed to enhance the spiritual experience, fostering a sense of sacred choreography.

5. Connection with Nature: Many spiritual spaces integrate the natural environment, recognizing the divinity inherent in the world around us. Gardens, courtyards, or elements that evoke natural landscapes contribute to a sense of harmony with creation. This connection with nature not only enhances the aesthetics but also serves as a reminder of the sacredness inherent in all aspects of existence.

6. Acoustics and Soundscapes: Sound plays a vital role in spiritual experiences. Architectural elements are designed to optimize acoustics, ensuring that prayers, chants, or meditative sounds resonate harmoniously within the space. The acoustic design enhances the auditory dimension of the spiritual journey, fostering a collective and transcendent experience.

7. Tranquility and Contemplation: Creating an atmosphere of tranquility and contemplation is central to the design of spiritual spaces. Architects employ materials, colors, and textures that evoke a sense of serenity. Quiet corners, meditation alcoves, or reflective pools provide individuals with spaces for personal introspection and communion with the divine.

8. Inclusivity and Openness: Modern spiritual architecture often emphasizes inclusivity and openness. Designs are conceived to welcome individuals from diverse backgrounds and beliefs. Inclusive spaces promote a sense of unity and shared humanity, fostering an environment where people of different faiths or spiritual traditions can come together in reverence and mutual respect.

9. Adaptability for Multifunctionality: Recognizing the evolving needs of contemporary worshipers, spiritual spaces are designed for multifunctionality. Spaces that can adapt to various rituals, ceremonies, community gatherings, and educational activities ensure that the spiritual center remains a vibrant and integral part of community life.

Expressing Spirituality through Architecture

1. The Cathedral: A Vertical Ascent: Cathedrals, with their soaring spires and expansive naves, epitomize the vertical ascent towards the divine. Gothic architecture, exemplified by structures like Notre-Dame Cathedral, employs pointed arches, ribbed vaults, and flying buttresses to create an awe-inspiring sense of height and upward movement. The play of light through stained glass windows adds a celestial quality, inviting worshipers to lift their gaze towards the heavens.

2. The Mosque: Symmetry and Unity: Mosques, rooted in Islamic architectural traditions, emphasize symmetry and unity. The focal point is the mihrab, indicating the direction of Mecca, while minarets stand as symbolic beacons. Geometric patterns, calligraphy, and tilework adorn mosque interiors, creating an atmosphere of order and beauty. The courtyard, as seen in the courtyard of the Great Mosque of Cordoba, provides a tranquil outdoor space for communal prayer and reflection.

3. The Temple: Harmony with Nature: Hindu temples, inspired by Vastu Shastra principles, seek harmony with nature. Temples are often situated along natural ley lines, and their designs incorporate axial alignments. Sculptures and carvings depict deities and mythological narratives, inviting worshippers to engage with sacred stories. Temples like Angkor Wat in Cambodia seamlessly blend with the surrounding landscape, creating a holistic and spiritually resonant environment.

4. The Synagogue: Sacred Geometry and Ark of the Covenant: Synagogues, influenced by Judaic traditions, often incorporate sacred geometry and symbolic elements. The Ark of the

Covenant, containing the Torah scrolls, serves as the focal point. Synagogue architecture emphasizes humility and introspection, with simple yet profound design elements. The Star of David, menorahs, and Hebrew inscriptions contribute to the sacred atmosphere.

5. The Meditation Center: Simplicity and Mindful Design: Meditation centers, irrespective of specific religious affiliations, often embrace simplicity and mindful design. The emphasis is on creating spaces that facilitate inner reflection and stillness. Minimalist aesthetics, muted color palettes, and uncluttered interiors contribute to an environment that invites individuals to turn inward and explore the depths of their own spirituality.

Contemporary Trends in Spiritual Architecture

1. Sustainable Design: A growing trend in contemporary spiritual architecture is the integration of sustainable design principles. Green roofs, energy-efficient lighting, and eco-friendly materials align with the spiritual ethos of stewardship for the environment. Spiritual spaces are increasingly seen as opportunities to model sustainability and environmental responsibility.

2. Interfaith and Multifaith Spaces: As societies become more diverse, there is a rising trend in the creation of interfaith and multifaith spaces. These environments are intentionally designed to accommodate various religious practices, fostering interfaith dialogue, understanding, and shared spiritual experiences. The emphasis is on unity and inclusivity.

3. Technological Integration: Spiritual spaces are incorporating technology to enhance the worship experience. Digital displays for religious texts, audio-visual aids for sermons, and online connectivity for remote participants are becoming more common. Technology is utilized thoughtfully to support, rather than distract from, the spiritual journey.

4. Adaptive Reuse of Sacred Spaces: Some architectural trends involve the adaptive reuse of existing sacred spaces. Abandoned churches or synagogues may be repurposed to serve new functions, such as community centers, art galleries, or educational institutions. This approach preserves the historical and cultural significance of the structure while giving it a renewed purpose.

5. Mindful Integration of Art: Art is increasingly being integrated into spiritual spaces as a means of expression and spiritual exploration. Sculptures, paintings, and installations contribute to the aesthetic and spiritual ambiance. Artistic elements serve as catalysts for contemplation and can convey spiritual narratives in innovative ways.

Challenges and Considerations

1. Preservation of Cultural and Historical Significance: Preserving the cultural and historical significance of spiritual spaces poses a challenge, especially in the face of urban development and demographic shifts. Striking a balance between modernization and the preservation of heritage requires careful consideration and collaboration with cultural preservation experts.

2. Accessibility and Inclusivity: Ensuring that spiritual spaces are accessible to individuals with diverse abilities and backgrounds is a critical consideration. Inclusive design, including ramps, elevators, and accessible facilities, contributes to a welcoming environment that accommodates the needs of all worshipers.

3. Balancing Tradition and Innovation: Architects and designers grapple with the challenge of balancing tradition and innovation in spiritual architecture. While honoring the timeless principles of sacred design, there is also a need to incorporate contemporary elements that resonate with modern worshipers. Striking this balance requires a nuanced understanding of both tradition and contemporary needs.

4. Environmental Impact: The construction and maintenance of spiritual spaces can have environmental implications. Balancing the spiritual significance of these spaces with sustainable design practices is a challenge. Architects are increasingly exploring eco-friendly materials, energy-efficient systems, and green construction methods to minimize the environmental footprint.

Summary

"Spiritual Spaces: Architecture for the Soul" explores the profound interplay between architecture and spirituality, highlighting the design elements and considerations that elevate physical structures into sacred sanctuaries. From the symbolism and sacred geometry embedded in traditional designs to the contemporary trends embracing sustainability and inclusivity, spiritual architecture remains a dynamic expression of humanity's quest for the divine. The chapter emphasizes the universal principles that underlie diverse spiritual traditions and the challenges architects face in preserving cultural heritage while adapting to the evolving needs of modern worshipers. Ultimately, spiritual spaces stand as transcendent monuments, inviting individuals on a journey of the soul, where architecture becomes a conduit for the sacred, fostering connection, contemplation, and the pursuit of the divine.

The Future of Holistic Architecture: Trends and Innovations

Holistic architecture, rooted in the philosophy of creating spaces that prioritize the well-being of individuals and the environment, is on a trajectory of continuous evolution. This chapter explores the emerging trends and innovations shaping the future of holistic architecture. From sustainable practices to technological integrations, architects are redefining the boundaries of design to create spaces that harmonize with the needs of the present and the aspirations of the future.

The Evolution of Holistic Architecture

Holistic architecture has undergone a remarkable transformation over the years, expanding beyond its initial emphasis on physical and environmental well-being to encompass a broader spectrum of human experiences. The future of holistic architecture is characterized by a synthesis of traditional wisdom, cutting-edge technology, and a heightened awareness of the interconnectedness between people, nature, and the built environment.

1. Sustainable and Regenerative Design: The emphasis on sustainability in architecture is not new, but the future of holistic design takes it a step further with a focus on regenerative practices. Architects are exploring designs that not only minimize environmental impact but actively contribute to the regeneration of ecosystems. Concepts like regenerative agriculture on rooftops, water harvesting, and materials that sequester carbon are becoming integral to holistic architectural practices.

2. Biophilic Design Integration: Biophilic design, which seeks to incorporate natural elements into built environments, is gaining prominence as an essential element of holistic architecture. The future sees a deeper integration of biophilic principles, with architects incorporating more green spaces, natural light, and elements that evoke a connection to nature. Living walls, indoor gardens, and natural materials contribute to an environment that enhances well-being and mental health.

3. Resilient and Adaptive Design: As the world faces challenges such as climate change and urbanization, the future of holistic architecture necessitates resilient and adaptive design strategies. Architects are exploring designs that can withstand environmental changes and adapt to evolving needs. Resilient architecture incorporates flexible spaces, modular construction methods, and considerations for extreme weather events to ensure long-term sustainability.

4. Technology-Enhanced Environments: The integration of technology is a driving force in shaping the future of holistic architecture. Smart building technologies, artificial intelligence, and the Internet of Things (IoT) are being leveraged to create environments that respond dynamically to the needs of occupants. Automated climate control, energy-efficient systems, and smart lighting contribute to a seamless and adaptive user experience.

5. Wellness-Centric Design: The future of holistic architecture places a heightened focus on designing spaces that actively contribute to the well-being of occupants. Architects are incorporating wellness-centric features such as circadian lighting systems, air purification technologies, and ergonomic design elements. Spaces are being crafted to promote physical health, mental well-being, and a sense of balance in daily life.

6. Modular and Prefabricated Construction: Addressing the need for sustainable and efficient construction methods, the future of holistic architecture embraces modular and prefabricated construction. These methods not only reduce construction waste but also enable faster and more cost-effective building processes. Modular designs provide flexibility for future adaptations and promote a more sustainable approach to construction.

7. Inclusive and Universal Design: Holistic architecture of the future prioritizes inclusivity and universal design principles. Spaces are being designed to accommodate individuals of all abilities, ages, and backgrounds. Inclusive architecture considers factors such as accessibility, sensory considerations, and diverse cultural needs to ensure that built environments are welcoming and supportive for everyone.

8. Cultural Sensitivity and Contextual Design: As the world becomes more interconnected, architects are recognizing the importance of cultural sensitivity in design. The future of holistic architecture involves a deeper understanding of local cultures, traditions, and contextual factors. Designs are curated to reflect the unique identity of the community, fostering a sense of place and belonging.

9. Collaborative and Community-Driven Design: Architects are increasingly adopting collaborative and community-driven design approaches. The future sees a shift from top-down design processes to inclusive methods that involve the community. Architects engage with end-users, local communities, and stakeholders to co-create spaces that meet the specific needs and aspirations of the people who inhabit them.

10. Net-Zero and Carbon-Neutral Buildings: The urgency of addressing climate change is shaping the future of holistic architecture towards the construction of net-zero and carbon-neutral buildings. Architects are exploring innovative ways to reduce energy consumption, utilize renewable energy sources, and implement carbon capture technologies. The goal is to create buildings that have a minimal or positive impact on the environment.

Innovations Shaping the Future

1. 3D Printing in Construction: 3D printing technology is making waves in the construction industry, offering a sustainable and efficient alternative to traditional building methods. Architects are exploring the use of 3D printing for creating complex and customized structures, reducing construction time and waste. This innovation has the potential to revolutionize the way buildings are constructed in the future.

2. Augmented and Virtual Reality in Design: Augmented reality (AR) and virtual reality (VR) technologies are being increasingly employed in the design and visualization stages of architectural projects. These technologies allow architects to create immersive experiences, enabling clients and stakeholders to virtually walk through spaces before they are built. This not only enhances the design process but also facilitates better communication and understanding of the final product.

3. Green Roofs and Vertical Farming: Green roofs, which involve growing vegetation on building rooftops, are gaining popularity as a sustainable design feature. Beyond environmental benefits, green roofs contribute to improved insulation and aesthetics. The future may see an expansion of green roofs and the integration of vertical farming systems into building structures, promoting urban agriculture and enhancing food sustainability.

4. Nanotechnology in Building Materials: Nanotechnology is making inroads into building materials, offering enhanced performance and sustainability. Nano-coatings can make surfaces self-cleaning, improve insulation properties, and provide resistance to environmental degradation. The use of nanotechnology in building materials aligns with the future goal of creating structures that are not only durable but also environmentally conscious.

5. Responsive and Adaptive Architecture: Advancements in materials and technology are enabling the development of responsive and adaptive architecture. Buildings can now dynamically respond to environmental conditions, adjusting their form and features based on factors such as sunlight, temperature, and occupancy. Responsive architecture contributes to energy efficiency and user comfort, aligning with the future goals of sustainable and user-centric design.

6. Biomimicry and Nature-Inspired Design: Biomimicry, drawing inspiration from nature to solve design challenges, is a growing trend in holistic architecture. Architects are studying natural systems and processes to inform design solutions. From mimicking the efficiency of natural ventilation systems to emulating the structural strength of biological organisms, biomimicry is shaping the future of sustainable and resilient architecture.

7. Flexible and Adaptive Interior Spaces: The future of holistic architecture envisions interior spaces that are flexible and adaptive to changing needs. Modular furniture, movable partitions, and smart interior systems allow spaces to be reconfigured for different functions. This adaptability aligns with the evolving nature of work, education, and social interactions, providing environments that can seamlessly accommodate diverse activities.

Challenges and Considerations

1. Balancing Technology with Human-Centric Design: While technology plays a crucial role in shaping the future of holistic architecture, there is a challenge in balancing technological advancements with a human-centric approach. Architects must ensure that technology enhances, rather than detracts from, the overall well-being and experience of occupants.

2. Ethical and Social Implications: The use of advanced technologies, data collection, and smart systems raise ethical and social considerations. Issues such as privacy, data security, and the potential for technology-driven disparities need to be carefully addressed to ensure that holistic architecture remains inclusive and equitable.

3. Global vs. Local Design Challenges: Architects face the challenge of navigating between global design trends and local contextual considerations. While global innovations offer valuable insights, it is essential to tailor designs to the specific needs, cultural nuances, and environmental conditions of local communities. Striking this balance requires a nuanced understanding of both global and local design challenges.

4. Education and Skill Development: The adoption of emerging technologies and sustainable practices in holistic architecture requires a shift in education and skill development within the profession. Architects need to stay abreast of technological advancements, sustainable design principles, and community engagement strategies to effectively contribute to the future of holistic architecture.

5. Regulatory and Policy Frameworks: The implementation of innovative and sustainable architectural practices relies on supportive regulatory and policy frameworks. Architects and policymakers must collaborate to create guidelines that encourage sustainable practices, incentivize green building initiatives, and address potential challenges related to new technologies and materials.

Summary

"The Future of Holistic Architecture: Trends and Innovations" explores the dynamic trajectory of holistic design, examining emerging trends and innovations that will shape the built environment in the years to come. From sustainability and wellness-centric design to technological integration and community-driven approaches, the future of holistic architecture is marked by a commitment to creating spaces that prioritize the holistic well-being of individuals and the planet. Innovations such as 3D printing, augmented reality, and biomimicry are redefining the boundaries of design, offering solutions that are not only environmentally conscious but also responsive to the evolving needs of diverse communities. As architects navigate challenges related to technology, ethics, and local-global dynamics, the pursuit of holistic architecture remains a transformative journey towards creating environments that foster harmony, well-being, and a sustainable future.

Case Studies in Holistic Architecture: Realizing Wellness in Design

The philosophy of holistic architecture extends beyond aesthetics and functionality to prioritize the well-being of individuals and the environment. Through case studies, we delve into real-world examples that exemplify the principles of holistic architecture, showcasing how thoughtful design can contribute to wellness in various contexts.

1. The Edge, Amsterdam: A Sustainable and Employee-Centric Workspace

The Edge in Amsterdam stands as a beacon of sustainable and employee-centric design. This innovative office space, designed by PLP Architecture, incorporates cutting-edge technology and environmentally conscious features. Rooftop solar panels generate energy, rainwater is harvested for reuse, and a smart lighting system adjusts to natural daylight levels, promoting energy efficiency. The interior design prioritizes employee well-being, with adjustable desks, ergonomic furniture, and a green atrium that enhances air quality. The Edge exemplifies how holistic architecture can create work environments that prioritize sustainability, energy efficiency, and the health of occupants.

2. Bosco Verticale, Milan: Vertical Forests for Urban Biodiversity

Bosco Verticale, or Vertical Forest, in Milan, Italy, redefines the concept of urban living by integrating nature into high-rise residential buildings. Designed by Stefano Boeri Architects, these twin towers are covered with lush greenery, including a variety of trees and plants. The Vertical Forest not only contributes to urban biodiversity but also improves air quality and provides natural shading, reducing the need for artificial cooling. This case study showcases how biophilic design principles can be applied on a vertical scale, bringing nature back into the urban fabric and enhancing the overall well-being of city dwellers.

3. The Spheres, Seattle: A Biophilic Oasis in the Corporate World

The Spheres, part of the Amazon headquarters in Seattle, Washington, exemplify the integration of biophilic design into the corporate setting. Designed by NBBJ, these spherical glass structures house a diverse collection of plant species, creating a lush and immersive indoor environment. Employees can use these spaces for work, meetings, or relaxation, fostering a connection with nature within the corporate context. The Spheres demonstrate how incorporating natural elements into the built environment can enhance the quality of workspaces and contribute to employee satisfaction and well-being.

4. T-House, Vietnam: Harmonizing Tradition with Modern Living

The T-House in Vietnam, designed by Vo Trong Nghia Architects, is a testament to the harmonious integration of traditional design principles with modern living. This residence embraces natural materials and local craftsmanship, incorporating a central courtyard that serves as a focal point for communal activities. The use of bamboo, a sustainable and locally sourced material, aligns with holistic principles. The T-House illustrates how cultural sensitivity, sustainability, and a connection to nature can coalesce to create a home that promotes well-being and a sense of place.

5. The Crystal, London: Sustainable Design for Environmental Consciousness

The Crystal in London, designed by WilkinsonEyre and Pringle Brandon Perkins+Will, is a sustainable and energy-efficient building that serves as a hub for urban sustainability. This case study highlights the importance of sustainable materials, energy-efficient systems, and integrated technologies in reducing the environmental impact of buildings. The Crystal features rainwater harvesting, solar panels, and energy management systems, showcasing how holistic architecture can contribute to the broader goal of environmental consciousness.

6. Singapore's Gardens by the Bay: Connecting People with Nature

Gardens by the Bay in Singapore, designed by Grant Associates and WilkinsonEyre, is a sprawling green oasis that integrates horticulture, sustainable design, and technology. This urban park features iconic Supertrees, vertical gardens, and conservatories that showcase plant life from around the world. The design promotes biodiversity, provides recreational spaces, and engages visitors in environmental education. Gardens by the Bay demonstrates how holistic architecture can create public spaces that not only enhance well-being but also foster a deeper connection between people and nature in an urban setting.

7. The WELL Building Standard: Prioritizing Health and Wellness

The WELL Building Standard is a performance-based system for measuring, certifying, and monitoring features of the built environment that impact human health and well-being. Case studies of buildings certified under the WELL Standard, such as the ASID Headquarters in Washington, D.C., showcase the integration of wellness-focused design elements. These include features like circadian lighting, air quality management, and initiatives promoting physical activity. The ASID Headquarters exemplifies how the WELL Standard can guide architects and designers in creating environments that prioritize the holistic health of occupants.

8. The Oasia Hotel Downtown, Singapore: Green Urban Retreat

The Oasia Hotel Downtown, designed by WOHA Architects, redefines the urban hotel experience by incorporating greenery into its design. The façade features a lush, permeable screen of red and green foliage that climbs the building, providing shade and promoting natural ventilation. The design prioritizes the well-being of guests by creating a green oasis in the midst of the urban landscape. The Oasia Hotel demonstrates how architecture can contribute to a sense of retreat and relaxation within the bustling urban environment.

9. The Living Building Challenge: Pushing the Boundaries of Sustainability

The Living Building Challenge is a rigorous certification program that goes beyond traditional sustainability by requiring buildings to be regenerative and restorative. The Bullitt Center in Seattle, certified under the Living Building Challenge, serves as a case study in pushing the boundaries of sustainable design. This commercial office building generates its own energy, collects and treats rainwater, and incorporates non-toxic materials. The Bullitt Center showcases how the Living Building Challenge can drive holistic architecture towards regenerative practices that actively contribute to the well-being of the environment.

Summary

"Case Studies in Holistic Architecture: Realizing Wellness in Design" provides a glimpse into diverse examples where the principles of holistic architecture are brought to life. From sustainable workspaces and urban green oases to residences that harmonize tradition with modernity, each case study illustrates the transformative impact of holistic design on the well-being of individuals and the environment. These real-world examples showcase the versatility and adaptability of holistic architecture, proving that thoughtful design can create spaces that not only meet functional needs but also nurture the physical, mental, and emotional well-being of those who inhabit them. As architects continue to draw inspiration from these case studies, the future of holistic architecture holds the promise of even more innovative, sustainable, and wellness-focused designs.

Table of Contents

Introduction to Holistic Architecture 2
The Intersection of Architecture and Well-being 4
The Power of Purposeful Design 6
Integrating Nature into Built Environments 8
Mindful Space Planning for Harmony 11
Biophilic Design: Enhancing Well-being with Nature 14
Sustainable Materials and Their Impact on Health 17
Light and Air: Optimizing Indoor Environments 20
Creating Tranquil Retreats within Urban Spaces 23
Harmony in Color: Aesthetics and Emotional Well-being 26
Acoustic Design for Serene Environments 29
The Role of Feng Shui in Holistic Architecture 32
Wellness-Centric Furniture and Interior Elements 35
Innovative Technologies for Healthy Living Spaces 39
Adaptive Reuse: Transforming Spaces for Well-being 42
Holistic Approaches to Urban Planning 45
Community-Centered Design for Social Well-being 48
Inclusive Design: Spaces for All Abilities 51
Cultural Influences on Holistic Architecture 54
The Impact of Architecture on Mental Health 57
Sustainable Landscaping for Holistic Living 61
Water Features and Their Calming Effects 65
Holistic Approaches to Workplace Design 70
Designing for Holistic Learning Environments 74
Spiritual Spaces: Architecture for the Soul 79
The Future of Holistic Architecture: Trends and Innovations 83
Case Studies in Holistic Architecture: Realizing Wellness in Design 87

Made in the USA
Monee, IL
10 April 2025